FEARLESS
CHURCH FUNDRAISING

FEARLESS
CHURCH FUNDRAISING

The Spiritual and Practical
Approach to Stewardship

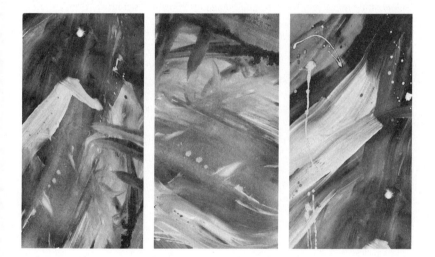

Charles LaFond

𝑀𝑃 | Morehouse Publishing
NEW YORK · HARRISBURG · DENVER

Morehouse Publishing, 4775 Linglestown Road, Harrisburg, PA 17112

Morehouse Publishing, 445 Fifth Avenue, New York, NY 10016

Morehouse Publishing is an imprint of Church Publishing Incorporated.
www.churchpublishing.org

Cover design by Laurie Klein Westhafer
Typeset by Beth Oberholtzer

Library of Congress Cataloging-in-Publication Data

LaFond, Charles D.
    Fearless church fundraising : the spiritual and practical approach to stewardship / by Charles D. LaFond.
        pages   cm
    Includes bibliographical references.
    ISBN 978-0-8192-2863-5 (book) — ISBN 978-0-8192-2864-2 (ebook)   1. Church fund raising.   I. Title.
    BV772.5.L34   2013
    254'.8—dc23
                                                                            2012042695

Printed in the United States of America

To Linda who taught me simply to be myself.

*To "Journey" Johnson who helped me to
become the fundraiser I have become.*

*To the Brothers of SSJE who taught me to be
the priest I had always hoped to become.*

*To my many friends who helped me become
the monk I had always hoped to become.*

*To the Episcopal Diocese of New Hampshire
in which I was taught to be the leader
I had always hoped to become.*

*And to Tom and Cheri Brackett who reminded
me along the way that honest, effective leadership
is lonely, powerful and generative.*

CONTENTS

ACKNOWLEDGMENTS

Having survived half a century as a priest, monk, solitary and fund-raiser, I feel grateful for the many people whose kindness and love have sustained my life and work. My mother taught me to find and claim my voice. My sister taught me to be right-sized. And my father, a writer by trade, forged in me the writer who is now emerging in this season of life.

He also gave me my first fountain pen and taught me to draw the ink up from bottle to pen and then, dripping one drop to the palm of his hand, said: "Son, be careful with this pen. That drop of ink can do great good or cause great harm. Be mindful every time you fill this pen with ink." I always have.

I acknowledge all those who bore Christ to me and taught me the power of God, who came to us not as the Idea, but as the Word. And so I am grateful to the many spiritual directors, professors and writers I have known, most especially the brothers of the Society of St. John the Evangelist in Cambridge, Massachusetts, in whose monastery I learned to love both learning and the desire for God.

This book is dedicated to many people whose hands spun it—like clay on the potter's wheel—into the vessel you now hold. Half a century ago, John Mark "Journey" Johnson hired me to lead fundraising and communications with the YMCA of Greater Richmond, Virginia. I had little experience but plenty of energy, creativity and desire. He was and remains the most Christ-like human I have ever encountered, and he taught me the value and compatibility of both Christ-centeredness and effective leadership strategy.

This book is also dedicated to Harold Hallock, with whom I served as a curate and in whose church I learned that one cannot be a prophet until one has first been experienced as a pastor. The plans we crafted together at Church of Our Saviour in Charlottesville, Virginia, were the seed from which this book grew.

Those seeds truly sprouted in my work with the Episcopal Diocese of New Hampshire, which asked me to lead stewardship in a state that is third in the nation for its wealth and dead last in the nation for its philanthropy. The feedback from the clergy, wardens and stewardship leaders in our forty-seven churches forged this book between the anvil of testing and the hammer of constructive feedback.

And finally, there are many people whose recent friendship made this book possible. Kevin Nichols, Margaret Porter and Judith Esmay companioned me in friendship and schooled me in ecclesial fearlessness. Jason Wells collaborated in ground-breaking work that crossed boundaries between evangelism and stewardship. Tom and Cheri Brackett's friendship modeled mutual deference, integrity, gentle power and right-relatedness to me, all of which are essential for a church that is, as Tom would say, molting into something fresh and new.

And finally I extend gratitude to Church Publishing Incorporated, Nancy Bryan and especially my editor, Stephanie Spellers, whose initial invitation, encouraging persistence and editorial skills midwifed my life's work into a tool that others can now use to help people blessed by raising money and those blessed by giving it away.

The Feast of St. Francis of Assisi, 2012
Blackwater Bluff Farm, Webster, New Hampshire

INTRODUCTION

According to the Hartford Institute for Religion Research there are about 350,000 religious congregations in the United States, and giving to religious institutions constitutes the largest and most stable percentage of all charitable giving in the United States.[1] Raising money in churches is clearly a big deal. The problem is that many churches nearly blow it, even though people are more likely to be generous to churches than any other institution asking them for money.

Major nonprofits like hospitals, universities and the YMCA (where I trained and discovered my vocation in stewardship) can afford full-time, energetic, talented staff who combine academic and scientific research with a passion for their cause. These fundraisers have local and national cohorts like the Association of Fundraising Professionals (http://www.afpnet.org/) to provide workshops, degrees and professional encouragement.

Compared to these professionals, most clergy and leaders of the churches, temples and mosques in America are sadly out of luck. They have never been trained in the one thing that will strengthen their congregation's mission resources, finance their ministry, fund their salary and likely shape their next job interview.

Clergy are trained in disciplines like ecclesiology, biblical studies and pastoral care. Just as critical is the ability to develop a strategic plan with measurable objectives, to manage a public awareness campaign that informs their communities about the congregation's mission, and to raise the money that keeps lights on and stoves cranking out pancakes on Shrove Tuesday or matzo during Hanukah.

I have a whole wall of textbooks on fundraising, communications, board leadership, branding, capital campaign design, planned giving and strategic planning. That is fine for a paid professional fundraiser. In my experience, churches need a one-stop book to get moving on raising money while attending to the intricacies of life in a community of faith.

---

1. http://www.hartfordinstitute.org/research/fastfacts/fast_facts.html#numcong, accessed 11/19/12.

This book was written to teach you how to effectively raise money, to reduce your fears about raising money and to provide the spiritual undergirding to raise and share money in a faith-based context. The fact is, raising money for a good cause is a life-giving activity that should be celebrated and enjoyed rather than shied away from and avoided. But we all need some help.

A Practical Approach

It is time to move well beyond the droning stewardship letter from the rabbi, pastor or rector. The church does not need another pledge card on a flimsy slip of paper with confusing boxes and vague, apologetic language that fits the envelope and pleases the treasurer but vexes the person filling it out. Strong fundraising requires prep work, research and follow-through. For many churches, there is a whole new paradigm to engage.

So we will not spend countless pages here telling you how much Jesus talked about money. Nor will we rehearse all the biblical references to giving or tithing or money. Instead, I hope to place effective tools in your hands so you can raise money well. We will also have some valuable conversation about how people think, why they give away their money, how they like to be asked for money and how you might shape your "case for support"—a fundraising term that answers the question "What will my gift do to change the world?"

This book attempts to provide a basic, no-frills, fool-proof path for raising an annual budget through pledges to a program or church. This is gimmick-free church fundraising. It is not a program; it is a basic recipe for success. It has been tested in hundreds of churches—rural churches with twelve members and urban churches with more than a thousand—and will prove useful whether you are leading a $12 million city-wide campaign or you are in a country parish raising an extra $10,000 for an exciting, new ministry.

This fundraising technology—spiritual and emotional, relational and technical—will work as well for an entire church as for a church group, as well for a YMCA as for a parochial school parent council. This material is designed so that any faith-based group can implement a plan to raise money without fear. Change certain language, images and artwork, and it could easily be used in another faith context.

I should offer this warning: If you try to use the material a la carte, you will be disappointed. Using a bit here and a bit there will work as well for you as using a bit of a recipe when baking. It all needs to be measured out, added and assembled. All of it.

To apply another metaphor, many things need to be working together in order for the seed you plant in the garden to thrive. The soil, the sunlight and the water all need to be right. And weeds, which rob the soil of valuable nutrients, need to be removed. Fertilizer (I use chicken poo at my farm in New Hampshire) needs to be applied in the right ways and at the right times. For a garden to produce the best crop of vegetables, it takes effective planning and hard work.

This book is a manual to get that job done at many levels. Along the way there will be humor, real-life stories, models of documents and even some encouraging preaching. If you are holding this book (in print or on a reading device), you have everything you need to walk into any church or small nonprofit, get the fundraising job done and help your plant to thrive.

A Spiritual Approach

"Many women were also there, looking on from a distance; they had followed Jesus from Galilee and had provided for him" (Matthew 27:55).

According to Matthew's gospel, Jesus received major gifts from the women who considered his ministry to be a good investment. Whether Jesus asked for this money or whether they simply gave spontaneous gifts we do not know. Based on the rest of Jesus' life and ministry, we can only assume that requests were made and ministry was funded.

Raising money is and has always been mission work and gospel work. It gets at our most basic instincts around scarcity and abundance, existence and the nearness of death. This work is challenging because, for fundraisers and donors alike, it is changing how we think and how we live, sometimes literally shifting neuropathways. But it is also moving us closer to the life and practice of Jesus.

The work we do in stewardship is not primarily about funding the budget of a church. Rather the work is about helping people to have an open relationship with Christ without guilt lurking in the shadows or shame hiding in the basement. God rejoices in our enjoyment of most of our money and simply asks that a portion be returned as a symbol. Just as a large or long-maintained financial debt with a close friend can get in the way of the friendship and joy of relationship, so too holding back on our pledge to God's ministry through our churches will get in the way of our relationship to God.

God has modeled this posture of generosity by giving the gift of a world and its resources into our care. God also gave God's own self away on the cross as the ultimate symbol of self-offering. We are made in the image of this same God who is creator, lover and giver. The extent to which we are all three of these is the extent to which we are living into God's hope for us all. When we dismiss the importance of sharing and raising money for the mission of the church, we are not only failing at fundraising. We are also missing the opportunity to help people engage in this work of creating, loving, giving and thus growing into the image of God.

Humanity is in a relationship with a God who gives to us all that we have. God asks us simply to give a part of it back, so that it is clear that we understand that everything we have is a gift from God. If we are hesitant to give a portion of our income to God through the church, the issue may not be greed, but good, old-fashioned fear. Will we have enough? Should we hold back the pledge? The healing of our stewardship programs—pledges, planned giving, major gifts, capital development and more—depends on our awareness that God loves us and that all we have is from God. Our pledge is merely a symbol of that awareness.

Fundraising without Fear or Apology

This book is titled *Fearless Church Fundraising* not because it takes so much courage to get the job done, but because knowing the basics will take the fear out of the task. In fearless fundraising, we are looking at the entire system, no matter how small the church or how fragile the congregation or how gifted the leadership. We are looking at not only how the money is being raised but also how the mission is decided, how the case is communicated and how the tasks of fundraising fit into the rest of church life. When we see this interconnected system clearly, there is no reason to fear.

Fear also manifests when leaders declare things like, "That is *fundraising* and we are doing *stewardship campaigns*." We try so hard to take the "fundraising" terminology and scrub it with the bleach of spirituality, desperate to get out the stink of "filthy lucre" (as the King James Version refers to money in 1 Timothy 3:3). Then we pack spices and herbs on it, gently rubbing in cinnamon, frankincense and myrrh with the hope that the term "fundraising," like the corpse of Jesus on Good Friday, will smell good and seem clean in its wrappings.

But the body that was nailed to the cross was not bad, it was just human—complete with its human smells. The same is true of the messy but real process in which we are engaged. What the donors are doing when they give a gift to a religious group may be an act of stewardship, but what we are doing in *asking* for that gift is fundraising.

All that said, we need not be so concerned about the term that we miss the point: coming to this ministry with a practical, spiritual and fearless approach. I hope this book helps to reduce fear and increase mission in the church.

## PART I

Fundraising and Giving as Spiritual Practice

## CHAPTER 1

The Joy of Giving: Growing Spiritual Gifts through Fundraising

Stop Battling and Start Abiding

All my life I battled being overweight, until one day I stopped dieting and began simply to change my relationship to food. The resistance to dieting was indeed giving energy to the cravings and the binges. One day I began to consider that food is wonderful and the body is a machine that needs some food and wants other food, and all those wants and cravings are based in the chemistry and biology of survival.

I finally stopped going on diets and counting calories—once the boney finger in my heart was replaced by a loving, open hand to life. Then, and only then, did my eating habits change and my weight stabilize.

I think the same can be true about our relationship with money. We can stop scolding ourselves and live peacefully and even joyfully with the bounty God has allowed us to enjoy. We can be intentional, make choices out of love rather than fear, imagine a way of life that creates more room for God and sets us on a path with Jesus. We can, in Jesus' words, begin to abide.

> As the Father has loved me, so I have loved you; abide in my love. If you keep my commandments, you will abide in my love, just as I have kept my Father's commandments and abide in his love. I have said these things to you so that my joy may be in you, and that your joy may be complete. (John 15:9–11)

When Jesus meets his disciples on the road and calls them to follow, the conversation is also about abiding. When they ask him, "Where are you staying?" they are not seeking an address. They do not want to know *where* he lives but *how* he lives. They want to know about abiding.

To simply live requires rather little attention. We get up, we wash, we eat, we defecate and urinate, we work, we rest. In fact I know plenty of people who are living. And living is okay. And there are times when surviving is all we can manage—abiding has to wait.

But as a way of life, abiding is very different. To abide is the art of living rather than the function of living. To abide, to live well and beautifully, takes attention to the ingredients of life. To abide takes special and regular attention to details like love, prayer, work, other people, giving time, giving talent and giving money away, receiving from others' generosity, giving and receiving kind words, walks in the woods, worship, vegetables, fruit, water, intimacy, friendship, fidelity and lots and lots of truth.

And where does generosity enter this recipe? Since we follow a Savior who gave himself away on the cross, giving what we have away to each other is essential. It is to the recipe of the Christian life, as flour is to the recipe of bread. Giving our selves away is the primary ingredient to abiding. I give an hour to God in meditation, another hour to my heart and mind in thought and a third hour to my body in exercise. The other twenty-one hours of each day grows out of my Rule of Life and in them I abide. When I first started out, I gave each five minutes. It's a process.

To abide is to live in God's bounty, to see God's bounty and to share God's bounty with a tired, hungry, cranky and hardened world. And the more we give away, the more clearly we will see all that God has given us and wants to give to us still. Our relationship to money and things changes, and we are free and blessed to finally abide.

Becoming Sméagol

Most of us, with some saintly exceptions, find pledging money to God, through the church, hard to do. I want to hold it back, let others pull my weight, rest on dead people's gifts to the endowment.

That is my inner-Gollum talking. Do you remember J. R. R. Tolkien's gnarled character in *The Lord of the Rings*? He had a split personality; "Sméagol" still vaguely remembered things like friendship and love, while "Gollum" was a slave to the Ring who knew only treachery, scarcity and violence.

One summer day I took a friend on a tour of my farm. She ooo'd and ahhh'd over a summer squash, and though my impulse was to pick it for her to take home, something inside me sputtered, crackled, chilled, hissed and withdrew. "I had a poor crop," a voice in my head said. "It is my preeeecious,"

Gollum might have said. That squash was the only one I could see. So I smiled, rather too sweetly, and we moved on.

The next day I was playing with my dog Kai and his ball went into the garden. Searching for it among the squash plants, I lifted leaves and found six huge gourds, more than I could possibly eat. It turns out that I could have shared with my friend. I chose not to do so.

Our pledge is not about giving to the church. Our pledge is about being who we were designed to be, trusting that we will have enough and giving some away. To practice giving is to practice letting go. Since we will all one day die, this practice is essential for human wellness.

When I give, I am leaning into the Sméagol part of my nature and away from Gollum. I am giving because I was designed in the image of a God who is creator, lover and giver. We give to God's mission through the church because we are seeking to live as redeemed and divine creatures, to reclaim the Garden of Eden, one square foot at a time. When I think, "I can't afford to give! I might need the money!," I go back to the work of Byron Katie whose methods of inquiry have changed my life and brought me to a renewed relationship with my thoughts and with truth.[2]

A Reconciling Ministry

Honest conversation about money can spur freedom and reconciliation: in ourselves, between us and our neighbors, between us and God.

I once had a housemate who was out of a job. I invited him to live in my guest-room and have the run of the house until he got back on his feet. My mortgage was $1,000 per month and I asked him to pay $150 per month (or 15 percent). He was grateful for the break and promised that, as soon as he had a job again, he would increase his share.

He paid his rent. He and his girlfriend would often have dinner with me, and we stayed up late laughing and talking about life. Our friendship deepened thanks to all the time and attention we gave to it.

A few months later, he found a job and bought new clothes and a new car with his new financial freedom. He never suggested that his rent go up, nor did I. In fact he paid half one month, saying that he would make it up the next month. The next month he forgot to pay the rent at all. He never again paid the full rent of $150, even though his income was higher than mine. Eventually he moved to a new home he bought across town.

Over the months before his move, as he stopped paying his full share, he tended to avoid me. He and his girlfriend never stayed for dinner and he

---

2. http://www.thework.com/index.php, accessed 11/19/12.

was usually gone when I came home and slept in long after I left for the office. Our friendship began to atrophy and die from malnutrition.

Years later he and I bumped into each other at a church conference. I suggested we meet for a beer. The conversation started out stiff and awkward until I said, "You know, I must have done or said something that offended you, because our friendship seemed to die before you moved out."

His eyes welled up and he said, "No, you did not do or say anything. It was me. I was so excited about my new job and was so busy dressing up to look the part that I had no money left over for the rent. The more I failed to pay the rent—which I knew to be only a fraction of what I should be paying—the more awkward I felt around you. I started to avoid you out of embarrassment. I saved a few bucks, but I destroyed our friendship."

I confessed that the gesture of using the house and not paying the rent made me feel a bit used. But the money was never really the issue for me; what I missed was the friendship. He apologized, I accepted his apology and now we are close friends. We laugh a lot these days.

No analogy about God is perfect, but this parable is the most apt description I can offer for what I see in our church and in our culture around stewardship. When I receive the bounty of this life—family, talent, land, money, safety, health, energy, food—as a result of God's creativity and generosity, and I give nothing back to God through the church, I begin to do what my housemate did. I begin to pull back from God, knowing that I am not keeping my part of a deal, a deal that is heavily weighted in my favor. I live a lie and my thoughts use shame to harm my heart. Shame says "I am a bad person." Indeed I am not. But healthy guilt says "I did a bad thing." Which is the start to living out our conversion. This book helps people out of financial shame, birthing guilt (mindfulness) into pledging and giving.

I can never truly repay the gift, but I can make a symbolic offering. It represents my understanding that what I have did not come from me but was a gift from God. No matter how hard I work for my salary, all of life is a gift from God. My pledge is simply a sign that I honor that relationship and reality and that I want it to flourish.

Free to Live and Give

My black lab, Kai, and I—like most families, I suppose—have a morning routine.

We get up around 5:00 a.m., and while I shower Kai goes off into the pasture to do what dogs do in pastures. Then I make coffee and get the fire going again. Kai sits in the kitchen by his bowl silently staring at me. When breakfast comes, Kai eats it. "Slurp, slurp, munch, munch . . ." His huge pink tongue licks his face. "Sigh."

I wish I could be as Kai is when he receives his food. He sits there, very peacefully, gently waiting for breakfast but never asking for it. He just waits there by his bowl. If I change the routine, he just waits longer but never objects. Never leaves that spot. Never makes a sound. And whatever I give him he eats happily. And when he is done, he bounds over to me after his sigh to rub his face on my leg in thanks.

I wish I could be that way with God. I wish I could just accept what I receive without worrying about getting more or having enough or being sure of what I get tomorrow. I wish we all could. It would free up our living and our giving.

## CHAPTER 2

The Fundraiser as Spiritual Leader

When it comes to money, the church has dirty hands. Reading nov-els like Ken Follett's *The Pillars of the Earth* or Susan Howatch's *Starbridge* series about the Anglican Church over the centuries, or watching recent television melodramas like *The Tudors* (about the sixteenth-century Angli-can Church), it is easy to see how manipulative the church has been about money. And the people in our pews have made the connection.

There is nothing we can do to change the reality that the church has, for centuries, used fear and intimidation to raise money for its structure and its buildings, often on the backs of illiterate peasants whose superstitions made them easy targets for manipulation. Monasteries and cathedrals charged pil-grims to see relics with supposed healing powers. Preachers frightened their parishioners with stories of demons torturing the damned with lava and pitchforks, knowing the congregation would pay big money to be released from their sins.

Those tactics do not work the way they used to, nor should they. A people living in fear will either give grudgingly or they will hold on to what they have for dear life, whereas a people who live in peace and joy will be more willing to part with what they have and share it with others. Fear curdles gratitude like lemon juice curdles milk. Unfortunately, we live in a church whose DNA is fear-based.

But this is a new day. The death of patriarchy has begun and with it may come a new form of Christianity—even a new form of society. As we heal and our perception of God moves from the perspective of a bad boy or girl standing in front of an angry and disinterested parent to being a good boy or girl standing in front of a loving and nurturing parent, our self-perception will change and our clenched fists will loosen on our money and our time. Fundraising and honest reflection on money and God heals us and heals our relationship with the church and with God.

The Fundraiser as Minister

What would stewardship and fundraising be like in our churches if we were to make the shift from fundraising being a nasty seasonal job to a ministry that helps people to be stronger Christians and better humans?

If you have ever been in a household with a teenager, you have seen the attitude some teens wear when doing their chores. Mom asks Joey to take out the trash and his whole body language tells the story—shoulders slump, a long, painful sigh oozes out of his pursed lips, his eyelids slide to half-mast, and his chin hits his chest. He stomps to the trashcan and pulls out the bag as if it is made of scalding lava. Then he plods to the garage as if the weight of the world were on his shoulders. It pulls the air out of the room and makes everyone around him miserable. And yet, to be a member of the family, he needs to be encouraged to do his part.

I think this is often what it feels like during campaign season in our churches. The leaders wince at having to raise money; they sulk at having to manage a dull and lifeless system (even sometimes a dull and lifeless liturgy). The members slump and their chins sink to their chests as they give their guilty offering, and the stewardship program ekes out its meager existence until the worst is over.

This need not be the case. Just as some doctors are joyful about the health they are bringing to the sick in a hospital, fundraisers in our churches can choose to be joyful about the ministry of helping people to be their best selves.

That may be easier said than done. For most of us, the idea of talking with people about their money and their giving is frightening and upsetting. There is a good reason: inviting people to release their grip on their money and to reconsider the level of their giving to the church, within the context of their relationship to God, touches on some very tender nerves. By improving stewardship campaigns, ramping up the conversation about money in order to change giving patterns, you will push many buttons and upset some people greatly.

It is only human for you to pull back from doing that, especially since you and they are in the same church and so are in a kind of family together. This is why so many people hate the notion of raising money in church and why stewardship campaigns are waylaid by procrastination. Procrastination is just resistance with a calendar attached to it!

Likewise, it is perfectly normal for clergy, whose salaries and benefits come from the money they are raising, to be squeamish about asking boldly for that money in a fundraising campaign. "Conversion of life" is often a term used for a moment of change such as an altar call or a public confession, however in its etymological sense conversion is simply the slow turning we do in life which reorients us away from sin and towards God. As I change my spending habits in order to make a larger pledge possible, I am as much in the process of conversion as if I were quitting smoking or moving from obesity to fitness. Conversion regarding stewardship is a slow process of improved choice-making around money. The only way to move forward is to remember that your work is conversion around money and the funding of mission, and not just asking for money.

The Fundraiser as Shepherd

The ministry of fundraising and the associated work of planning and communications is holy—not because it is called "stewardship," but because it helps people to know how to live well. It is important because it reduces their fear and shame around money and God.

People know they need to give their money away. People know they are only shopping and consuming in order to anesthetize their fears. They know the flourishing of their church depends, in part, on money, and they know the money comes from people who attend the church and consider it their community.

But when it comes to money, the people in our pews are, as scripture says, sheep wandering without a shepherd. The one thing we manage and touch every day—money—is the one thing we are anxious about discussing boldly. The one thing about which we are most afraid—having money—is the one thing that we so often fence into the four weeks of a poorly run stewardship or annual fundraising campaign. The one subject in which we need real logistical and spiritual help—financial stewardship—is the one that we leaders are likely to discuss only superficially and with hesitation.

That has to change, because people need to be freed, and only the gospel and the giving away of our lives, and sharing of our possessions, will save us.

I think of doing solid, effective fundraising as something akin to rescuing people from sure disaster or pointing out a leading star in a dark night sky. In fact, the two are one and the same. The word "disaster" was coined in the Middle Ages by combining two words: *dis* or "without," and *astron*, or "star." To be "dis-astron" referred both to the danger of a ship at sea that could not see and navigate by the stars in a cloud-covered and stormy sky; and to the star of Bethlehem, which guided humanity to the source of salvation lying in the manger. Nautically, to be without a star could mean death. Spiritually, to be without the star announcing Jesus' birth could mean another kind of death.

People today suffer a modern spiritual "disaster." It is rooted in our troubled relationship with money, and it manifests in over-stimulation, over-spending and good old-fashioned greed. Television says we are fat—so we buy diet pills and exercise equipment. Television says we are plain—so we buy more and more clothes to feel impressive. Television says terrible things will happen—so we buy more pills and more insurance. Television says we are boring—so we buy new and bigger toys, cars, houses, gadgets.

But here is the truth: Television is lying to us. Television and other advertising are playing on our fears and our inadequacies in order to get us to spend our money. Why was there so much advertising for home insurance in the months after Hurricane Katrina and so many commercials for life insurance after the terrorist attacks of 9/11? TV capitalizes on our deepest fears and cranks out three or four lies and temptations every minute, all evening long. The light coming out of that box is not the true light; it is just the blue light.

The ministry of stewardship is a pastoral ministry to a people who are being bludgeoned by advertising and cultural forces rooted in fear. It is a star that helps us to navigate in darkness and guides us to our destination. It is as if we are moving in the wee hours of the morning during the Great Vigil of Easter, growing the light as candles are lit one to another to another and then carried out into the world. It is the light of Christ leading us all from fear to grace.

The Fundraiser as Presence-Maker

The moment when Jesus hangs on the cross, his mother, Mary Magdalene, Mary the wife of Cleopas and John all stand with him in silence. It is one of the most frequently rendered and beautiful moments in scripture. What the Marys and John are doing with Jesus is presence-making. They are simply standing with Jesus as he does what he is called to do. That presence-making is part of the "good" of "Good Friday."

As people helping the church with stewardship and fundraising, your job is that very same presence-making. You are called to be present with people as they learn to give their money away. You are asked to provide the stewardship campaign that will help people to ask hard questions about their money, their God, their faith, their shame, their greed, their vulnerabilities, their fears, their freedoms. That will be hard ground to stand on, but stand you must.

As you go about helping people to give their money away, understand that the anger, frustration and resentment firing your way are not actually meant for you. People will scapegoat you as they spin and struggle. Your job is to repeat the mantra, "This anger is not about me." Your job is to be present. Imagine that you are holding a small child having a temper tantrum. You hold her tightly even as she pounds your chest with her small fists, trusting that eventually she will stop crying from either exhaustion or peace. Sadly, adults are not much different when it comes to our fears and even our tantrums. We strike out, often at those who are trying to help us.

Being honest about this pattern helps fundraisers to weather the rough patches and bear the bruises our communities may inflict. Knowing this truth helps us to stay present as members do the hard work of bringing what they say they believe in line with how they live and how they spend their money. People want that alignment, but the process of getting there is painful. As presence-makers, we accompany them on that journey.

The Fundraiser as Coach

The fundraiser or stewardship campaign chairperson often shrivels into the role of "the beggar" or "the nagger" or "the scolder." I would suggest we shift that self-understanding and see ourselves as "the coach." Think of a coach as someone who stands with people as they do hard, internal work; this time, it is the work of reorienting their minds, hearts and souls regarding money and Christian life.

I am grateful for the coaches in my life. When I was working at the YMCA, I was about thirty pounds overweight. In my twenties, I was a financial development officer for one of the nation's largest metropolitan YMCAs. As vice president, I oversaw the communications, marketing and development activities for a dozen YMCAs, a camp and conference center and thirty-nine child-care facilities. I tended to move fast, sleep little, work long and eat badly. And even though walking through the front doors of the downtown YMCA with a McDonald's bag was like crossing an angry picket line, I packed on the pounds.

My boss, an encouraging and gentle man, encouraged me to take better care of myself. So one day I met with a fitness trainer from the downtown YMCA and asked for help. He listened with deep compassion and strength. He explained the basics of weight-loss exercise and got me going on a treadmill. We were on level one and after only ten minutes I was willing to confess to just about anything if he would let me off the machine!

Every day my fitness trainer met me at 12:10 p.m. at my reserved treadmill. He programmed and started the machine. Every day I ran and ran.

Gradually he increased my speed and stamina, even as I decreased my visits to the McDonald's drive-thru. Those early days were hard and painful, but he told me time and again that I was doing well. He literally kept me moving.

Months later I was thin again. My fitness trainer, whom I hated at first for making me do what I said I wanted to do, never left my side. He coached, encouraged, cajoled, and presenc-ed me into doing the hard work of aligning my body, spirit and values.

Similarly, a good church fundraiser—lay or ordained—is a coach. Like my fitness instructor, these leaders help people in their churches to do a hard, counter-cultural thing. At first people will be as I was on that treadmill: they will moan and groan and some will even hate you for coaching them to give their money away. They may resent you for ramping up the rhetoric about giving.

Just as I was short-tempered with my fitness instructor when he increased the speed of my treadmill, your congregants may be short-tempered with you as you move from a weakened, budget-centered stewardship season to a healthy conversation about money, giving, standards of living, choice-making, rule of life and the many other factors which go into a robust stewardship campaign.

If you stay the course, you will see people becoming stronger. They will start giving more as you get better at asking for money, telling the church's story and thanking people for giving. Donors will be transformed; your resources for mission will also be transformed, sending the smiles out in rings around your church like concentric circles flowing from a stone tossed in a pool.

That fitness trainer did only one thing. He stood there. He waited with me just as John, Jesus' mother and the other women waited with Jesus on the cross. He told me I could do it when I thought I could not. Why would it be any less hard for a society engulfed in self-centered spending, debilitating debt, wracking fears and relentless media encouragement to spend, spend, spend? Why would the members of that society find it easy to give their money away to God or to anything or anyone else?

▪▪

## CHAPTER 3

Fear, Resistance and Acedia: Removing Spiritual Blocks to Giving

There are countless allied forces arrayed and working to prevent our generosity and gratitude. Have you ever noticed that the "seven deadly sins" all involved stewardship, possessions and giving, each in its own way?

Luxuria:	(extravagance or lust) warping God's gifts
Gula:	(gluttony) stealing God's gifts from others
Avaritia:	(greed) hoarding God's gifts
Acedia:	(sloth or spiritual depression) sitting on God's gifts
Ira:	(wrath) being blinded to God's gifts
Invidia:	(envy) wanting more than God's gifts
Superbia:	(pride) not recognizing one is not God

These deadly sins are a powerful lot. I have identified three other challenges that surge to the surface during stewardship and fundraising: resistance, fear and acedia (or spiritual boredom). For those who are leaders in the work of fundraising, a lack of self-awareness around these intertwined forces is a dangerous Achilles' heel. In this chapter, we will take some time getting to know each of these forces, how they emerge, how they intertwine and how they can be healed.

On Fear

If there is only one aphorism for which I would like to be known it is this: "We are not greedy people. We are scared people. Greed is just the way we choose to scream in this culture and at this time in history."

Why are we so very afraid? And what does that fear have to do with raising money in church or giving money away?

When we are afraid, we turn inward. Like the armadillo, the turtle, the centipede, the snail, we tend to pull inward. Have you ever tried to walk across a high bridge or along a ledge without a railing? Have you noticed the way your body freezes and turns inward in fear? We become small, we pull in our appendages and we shrink back. Jesus knew that about us, which is why he so often urged his disciples, "Do not be afraid."

Fear tends to cause us to white-knuckle our money as a form of security. In the parable of the Rich Young Ruler (Mark 10:17–22), the ruler asks Jesus what will bring eternal life. In other words, he wants to know what will guarantee him security, safety and wellness forever. Jesus recites the laws of Torah: no murder, no stealing, no sex outside marriage, no lying and be nice to your parents when they get on your last nerve. The man says he does all that.

Jesus sees beyond the presenting symptoms to the deeper illness. This man is not worried about being happy in the afterlife. He is worried about this life. And then occurs, in my opinion, one of the most tender moments in scripture: "Jesus, looking at him, loved him."

The word for "love" here is not *phileo* but rather *agapeo*. A better translation might be, "Jesus looked straight at him; his heart warmed to him." Jesus saw past what he feared to what he lacked—and what he lacked was a peaceful heart.

We modern Americans, together, own more possessions today than every person today and stretching back to the earliest days of human history *combined*. Those of us in Western, developed nations own more things than every human on earth now and since the world's creation.

Our grasping at possessions is a way of acting out our fear. "I own this. I have power over this thing. I appear to have it all together because I have these things. People will think well of me if I have these things." I have swallowed that hope hook, line and sinker. And I know I am not alone.

It is essential that we have a good understanding of the cultural, religious and emotional setting in which our congregants live so that we understand how best to proceed in the ministry of fundraising. Most churches are using methods for fundraising that worked well in the 1950s when television shows like *Leave It to Beaver* accurately depicted the way many Episcopalians lived. Today, we need different technologies and skills for courageous fundraising. And chief among those is an understanding of the nature and function of fear in our lives.

American people are not greedy. They are busy and they are scared. I have seen it in meetings with newly appointed stewardship and fundraising committees in small churches. It can feel like stepping into a refrigerated funeral parlor. The fear hangs in the air like smoke. Each person on the committee loves his or her church, but each also brings at least two layers of fear into the room.

There is a reason that Jesus spoke so much about money and so often about not being afraid. It is because they are so often linked. An American has only to peek through our carefully constructed international fences to see the misery our wealth and standards of living create across this globe. We are molten with fear that the precarious house of cards in which we live will one day fall.

Making a financial pledge to one's church or area nonprofit is a scary thing, precisely because we are not sure that one day we might not need that money. This fear need not paralyze us as we prepare pledge campaigns. But it should remind us that we are on holy and rocky ground when we talk to over-stimulated, over-caffeinated, over-worked, and deeply fearful people about giving their money away.

Healing the Fear

The effective church fundraiser must face and manage numerous fears in order to be successful in facilitating conversion and raising money for mission. And it starts with the fundraisers themselves.

As leaders, we are often afraid regarding our own personal giving and money issues. "*Am I giving enough? I wish I had more to give. Will people find out what I give? Am I a hypocrite not to be giving more? I give one and a half percent, and since the mill closed I can barely feed my family. What if we start talking about the tithe? Then what do I do?*"

The second layer of fear in the room centers on providing leadership around one of the most nerve-wracking subjects in the life of the church. Faith-based fundraising leaders constantly ask themselves questions like: "*Will my friends in this church dislike me for leading a campaign that is asking them to give? Are we really making a difference or am I raising money for the perpetuation of a club? Do people know what I pledge? Everyone seems to have money problems, so can we raise money in a more indirect way, like bake sales and spaghetti dinners? What if my team does not raise this money?*"

There are personal and corporate fears, any of which can send a fundraising leader into paralysis. I have seen fundraising committees spend whole meetings on letters and logos, on mission statements and special event planning, only to find that they were using busy-work to mask their very real, personal anxiety around actually raising the money.

When I am beginning work with a group or congregation regarding fundraising or stewardship, I often begin by asking them to engage in an exercise. I break them up into pairs and invite them to reflect on and discuss their first memory in which fear and money met. The same exercise is also a fine way to engage a congregation in the place of a stewardship sermon. Until we know what we are afraid of we cannot make friends with the fear.

A Story of Fear

Here is my story about the intersection of fear and money:

When I was a boy, my mother and I went to London with my father on business. I was eight years old and had just been to Hamley's Toy Store. I found a computerized version of the old plastic Battleship game, designed to allow one player to play alone against the machine. It featured sounds like torpedoes and explosions, and it seemed like a godsend to an eight-year-old sentenced to live for weeks on end in a London hotel. I had the money for the game in my pocket. It was a month's allowance for a European trip.

My mother was silent as I purchased the game. She only once said, in a gunmetal-gray tone of voice, "Are you *sure* you want to spend all your money on this *one* game so early on the trip, my darling?" I was certain.

That is, until we came to a stop sign near Hyde Park. My mother tapped my hand and gestured out the window of the cab. There, standing on the corner, was a street person. He was huddled on cardboard and wore tattered, black and brown clothing. He looked right at me, and my mother said, "If you keep spending money like you did on that game, that beggar will be you one day."

In that moment I became afraid of money and struck cold with the vulnerability of not having it.

Early experiences like mine can tell us a lot about what kind of emotional and psychological programs are running within our computer minds— draining energies and dragging efficiency. By taking congregants through an exercise in which they practice "mindfulness" around money, you help them to see the old roots of fear. And anyone who has ever tried to uproot an ancient tree with a deep root system knows it is hard work.

On Resistance

Resistance comes from two words meaning "against" and "to take a stand." It is a twelfth-century word, but it is surely an ancient human attribute and common part of spiritual life. In fact, spiritual direction—the act of caring for the spiritual life of another person through spiritual conversation— nearly always wrestles with resistance.

As a monk at the Society of Saint John the Evangelist in Cambridge, I spent many an hour with clergy and guests doing spiritual direction. It was a tremendous honor to be invited so deeply into the intimate thoughts of people trying to live a good, Christian life. When the spiritual director sits with his or her directee, the job at hand is simply to have a conversation about how life—in particular, the spiritual life—is going.

But what any trained spiritual director knows is to always be on the lookout for resistance. For the spiritual director, when resistance pops up, it is a red flag waving and announcing, "There is anxiety here! Pay attention to this subject!" The skilled director will note the subject and gently return to it to try to get to the root causes of spiritual distress.

The same pattern operates in any human relationship. My mother always became agitated and short-tempered during a rain storm. She would snap at me and my dad over the smallest things when it was raining. That was only the presenting issue.

Years later, I was sitting with her during a thunderstorm. The frail woman before me was still upset by the thunderstorm, but she was too sick to transfer that fear into anger. Instead she just reached out and took my hand. When I asked what the problem was, she finally told me what it was like, sixty years earlier, to be eight years old in an air-raid shelter underground while German planes dropped bombs on her London neighborhood during the Blitz.

Night after night the earth shook around her, and morning after morning she emerged to see whose homes had been burned or demolished by bombs. With my hand still in hers, she looked up at me with red, watery eyes and reminded me that "blitz" is the German word for lightning. All of a sudden my mother's erratic, violent behavior during thunderstorms made sense. There was a story behind her resistance; I just had to listen for it.

So the question is this: why do people in church react so strongly about money? Why can perfectly sane people spend money on all sorts of useless, plastic, nylon things at Wal-Mart or purchase enormous televisions but stiffen when money comes up in the context of church? If we can go deeper than just the presenting issues, then we can begin to diagnose the illness and not just the symptoms.

Symptoms of Resistance

The surface symptoms of resistance we commonly see when raising money in church are many, but here are some I have noticed:

- Members avoid any discussion of money. "Don't talk about it. Just send me my pledge card."
- If you preach about money, people lodge charges of everything from poor taste to manipulation.

- When asked for money, congregants often play the "stewardship-is-more-than-money card." They cite the *time* they give to the church or the care they take in recycling and stewarding the environment—anything but a discussion of money.
- Budget conversations become quickly heated, the stage on which people's pathologies play out. Money in the church budget gets scapegoated when what people are really worried about is their personal finances.

In church leadership we too often and too quickly look at symptoms like these—we might call them "acting out"—without seeking root illnesses. Could it be there are unhealed resentments about the last rector who was a narcissist, megalomaniac and womanizer? Could it be that people feel they are not receiving the care they need, or that they are not being heard, and it is coming out as anger or dissatisfaction? Could it be that coercive power, manipulation, mismanagement, shallow spirituality or buried congregational conflict is the reason people resist the annual stewardship pledge campaign? They should resist. It may be the only way for the congregation to say there is a problem.

On the other hand, much resistance will simply come from people overspending, not having a realistic budget, responding to too much bad news in the media or simply lacking the spiritual maturity to live with gratitude and give back to God what is God's. Sometimes narcissism and grudges are getting in the way.

At root, I believe we sense resistance around money because we are ashamed. Rich and poor among us—we are all ashamed and insecure about what we have, and we are all afraid of not having more or, at least, enough. How much is enough? More than we will need. How much will we need? We do not know.

Responding to Resistance

When I go to a church and watch a sermon about money and giving, I am always fascinated by the congregation's body language. Legs cross. Arms fold. Eyes move to the floor. Heads lower. Bodies shift into pew side-saddle sitting so that the preacher is preaching to left shoulders. There is a silent struggle.

The usual, emotional response to resistance like this is to increase intensity. The preacher or speakers will subconsciously increase their speed, increase their volume, open hands to each side of a pulpit in order to broaden their chest and sometimes radiate anger back out to the congregation.

Imagine if we responded in these ways instead:

Responses to Resistance

Replace this response	With this response
loud	clear
"you are stewards for an absent God"	"you bear Christ into this world with money as a tool for good"
intense	gentle
club dues	ministry investment
raising money	deserving money raised
anger	compassion
imploring	invitation
"God wants . . ."	"people need . . ."
"I give because . . ."	"I love this church because . . ."
scolding	thanking
a charge of greed	a call to action

Resistance is as old as Moses, literally. There will be differing reasons for it, but be assured that the deeper the spirituality of the congregation, and the better the case for support and campaign management, the less resistance you will encounter.

And when resistance comes, as it surely will, recall that becoming reactive is never the answer. Leaders should see resistance, like conflict, as a natural occurrence that simply needs to be met with the strength that comes from centered, kind and loving leadership. What is essential is to let no one hold hostage the spiritual growth of the congregation. No matter how rich, how influential or how loud they are or how long they have been there, no one should have power to prevent the congregation doing work that is so critical to their conversion-of-life.

The best way to deal with resistance around raising money is to face it with bold clarity and humor. There is nothing cranky Episcopalians hate more than having their bile responded to lovingly and kindly with humor. And when you remain firm in your determination to have the fundraising conversation in your church, you will find the resistance breaking into relief.

The response reminds me of an intervention: those close to a person with addiction will gather in the living room. Mother, father, parish priest or minister, close friends, a counselor . . . they all gather like a somber surprise party in a silent room.

When the addicted person walks in and realizes that he or she has walked into an intervention, there is a mingling of both fear and relief. There may be fear. "How could these people turn on me? How will my life change without the self-anaesthetizing effects of my substance of choice? Can I stand to feel the pain of life for a while?" Alongside those fears, there is also huge relief. "The pretense that 'everything is okay' is finally over. No one was fooled. It was just a huge conspiracy of silence. Now the silence is broken, and I can start to heal."

The changes to a church's life when it is overcoming resistance may be painful, but the resulting balance will feel right and good. That has been our experience in the Diocese of New Hampshire. We have been shocked to actually be talking about money, a subject we had tried to ignore or to pretend no one needed to talk about. But in our hearts we know that living in wealth—even relative wealth—while the world starves is not right, and we are glad to know the gig is up. We know that shopping as a way to relieve stress and dull pain and despair is not the way to live, and we are glad that we have begun a spiritual and financial intervention.

Leadership in the church must gather people with loving kindness and help them to do the right thing. We must accept the frailty, guilt and vulnerability of our fellow humans as they struggle with money and their response to God regarding it.

On Acedia

Acedia or spiritual boredom is a strong poison that can sicken the most thoughtful stewardship program. Acedia is a technical term in Christian spirituality, and it signifies joylessness, weariness, boredom, listlessness and, at its worst, a spiritual depression which clouds the mind and dulls the heart.

With acedia, nothing is "bad"—exactly—it is just that nothing seems good either. Psalm 91 refers to this sensation as "the pestilence that stalks in darkness, or the destruction that wastes at noonday." As Bill Stafford puts it, "Accidie, or spiritual boredom, is the eagerness of many Christians to *endorse* the *idea* of spiritual discipline alongside their disinclination to *actually do anything*."[3]

The danger of acedia is that it is so like depression that you may not know you have it. Like alcoholism, the more drunk you are, the less likely you are

---

3. William S. Stafford, *Disordered Loves: Healing the Seven Deadly Sins* (Cambridge, MA: Cowley Publications, 1994), 114

to realize you are drunk. Similarly, the more spiritually depressed you are, the less likely you are to see the depression.

Acedia results in a dull pain, not a sharp one. The person, family, group or organization suffering from acedia will simply become immune to the blessings around them. For a person with acedia, the sun is too bright, the water is too wet, the day is too long, the hours are passing too slowly, and the apple is never sweet enough. It is the spiritual equivalent to riding in beautiful farmland with a blindfold on.

Acedia and Stewardship

What does acedia or spiritual depression have to do with stewardship and leadership in our churches? On a practical level, it plays out when people build a fantasy, cloak themselves in nostalgia, or simply self-anesthetize to escape reality. That stuckness can wreak havoc with a church's ability to raise money effectively.

When, for example, a church leadership team hides behind nostalgia ("Things were better when Father Damian was here . . .") or fantasy ("True, John has never managed an effective campaign before, but it would hurt his feelings to change chairs, and this year things will be different . . ."), they slip into lack of mindfulness and dull self-delusion.

When acedia or spiritual boredom comes along—and it will from time to time—it shadows all things like a cloud. This spiritual depression unplugs the power that generates gratitude. Take away gratitude (which is a form of being present), and stewardship is going to die or be debilitated.

In a congregation, this kind of corporate depression or acedia develops out of a low level of spiritual vitality, either in the clergy or lay leaders or both. Just as a marathon runner who does not run will soon become a couch potato, so a priest or lay leader who does not pray will soon become enveloped in acedia. The power of well-rested, well-prayed, centered, healthy clergy and lay leadership cannot be underestimated. A church may have the most efficient managers in its leadership and the finest fundraisers leading on stewardship, but if the church is spiritually shallow, then stewardship will be infected with discontent. That inevitably leads to the murmuring (or complaining) Saint Benedict warned his monastic communities to avoid at all costs.

Digging out from Acedia

The prescription to heal acedia is the same as that which is prescribed to the depressed person: Get out there and do something. Notice what is around you. Be grateful. And if there is a remedy for the congregation suffering acedia, it is to become spiritually vital, fostering engagement, deep awareness and gratitude.

Giving has much more to do with spiritual depth than it does the desire to fix a broken world. This is why churches doing lackluster teaching and formation are never going to reach their potential around stewardship. It is why fundraisers who are not grounded in spirituality will always be rowing upstream.

What would we see if we were to dig deeper into the wells of our spiritual lives? What would it look like?

First of all, there would be rigorous awareness and truth. I actually define spirituality as a relentless seeking after and expressing of truth. It is the opposite of nostalgia, which is merely the lies of the past, or fantasy, which is the lies of the present and future. To sit in truth, no matter how painful, is to welcome the Holy Spirit to enter and convert us slowly but surely.

Giving Is the Answer

There may be no better antidote for acedia than the joy of giving. Science proves it.

Recently, New Hampshire Public Radio's *As It Happens* reported on a discovery regarding the workings of the human brain.[4] The study employed advanced mapping of the brain to examine the impact of giving money away.

Whenever we do or see or feel things—for instance, sadness or fear—various areas of the brain become active with special electrical charges. In this medical study, people were given the opportunity to designate charities for auto-debits from their paychecks. The electrodes attached to their heads showed which parts of the brain "lit up" or became active when they made their pledges.

The scientists expected that the standard "giving" or "kindness" parts of the brain would light up. They were surprised to also trace activity in the area reserved for *receiving* a gift. In other words, when we *give* our money away our brains experience giving as if we had *received* a gift. Scripture tells us that giving feels good and builds energy in a community, but science just proved it.

In this study, even people who were giving to a charity they did not know or care about still displayed subconscious impulses which lit up areas of the brain reserved for activity when we *receive* a surprise gift.

---

4. New Hampshire Public Radio, As It Happens [radio program], "The objectivism of their disaffection: Neuroscientists prove that humans are hard-wired to commit un-Ayn-Randian acts of kindness," June 4, 2007.

The second area of the brain to activate was the one usually sparked upon intimate encounter with a close friend. In other words, every time a person checked a box designating some of their money to a charity, the same spot in the brain reserved for intimate friendship encounters would light up. Even if the charity was unknown to the giver—even if they were just picking from a list of charities—the brain experienced that act as an encounter with a friend.

One of the challenges of parish stewardship programs is that we think people do not want to give or be asked to give; we are afraid it will drive people who were already ambivalent further away. Sometimes that is true for a small number of people. But our ministry of helping people to give is focused on opening people to experience joy and satisfaction and pleasure, all of which really do come from giving.

Leaders on the Frontline

I end this section with a charge to the stewardship and fundraising leaders on the frontline: please take special care of your spiritual life so that you are open to the workings of God's co-creativity. I am convinced that we are dealing not only with a loving God who wants us to heal around issues of money and fear; we are also dealing with all sorts of evil that seek to get in the way of our work.

The church leader dealing with issues around money must tend his or her own spiritual garden. Regular discursive prayer, meditation, spiritual direction, time in silence and reflection and good self-care of the mind and body are all essential for anyone seeking to navigate the choppy waters where money and church flow together.

The key to church leadership is linking effectiveness and skill with faithfulness to God. Pray for the mountain to be moved . . . but bring your shovel. Ask God to raise the money you need to do ministry, but then be open to the creative movements of the Holy Spirit seeking to help you to get this job done.

And finally, please internalize this single truth: there already exists all the money you need to do the ministry to which you have been called. Now all you need to do is create a system that effectively moves those resources from the people's pockets into the community's hands.

There is an old Jewish story about an old, blind, childless, poor man fishing on a river's edge near Jerusalem, joined by Elijah. The blind man senses Elijah sitting there, welcomes him and asks why he has come. Elijah says he has come from God to offer one wish—but only one. Any wish he wants and God will grant it.

"Oh my," says the old blind man, "what shall I ask God to give me!? I am blind and so I should like to see. I am childless and so I would love the security and joy of small children in my home. I am poor and would like to provide my wife with some small financial security. I do not know what to wish for. I must ask my wife!" So they agree to meet at the same place, same time the next day.

The old blind man asks his wife, "What should I ask of God?" She thinks and smiling, places her hand on his and leans in to whisper in his ear. His face lights up.

The next day the old man meets Elijah at the same place along the river fishing. He says to Elijah that it was a hard decision, since he so desired three things: to see, to have children and to be financially secure. Elijah nods and reminds him he can only have one wish.

After consulting again with his wife, the man returns. "Here is my one wish: That I might see my children eat off of gold plates!"

We have to be wise, bold and honest in how we approach God, and help our congregations to do it, as well. But if we are, we can share God's bounty with a tired, hungry world.

PART II

Getting Practical about Fundraising

CHAPTER 4

■■

Essential Leadership Practices

We can move towards a deeper and more vibrant conversation in the church about money and giving, and help our congregations to heal and mature, by engaging in three comprehensive practices:

1. Be effective and kind, not necessarily nice, leaders.
2. Nurture vibrant spiritual, organizational and worship life.
3. Deserve the money you are trying to raise.

Let's take them one at a time:

Be Effective and Kind, not Nice

The conversation we have must be a kind one and an effective one, and not just a shallow, word-veneered, "nice" one. In church leadership, I use this formula to manage these distinctions:

$$\text{Effective} - \text{nice} + \text{kind} = \text{good leadership}$$

Why "effective"? One of the problems we face in church fundraising is that we get tied up in knots, get nervous about relationships and feelings and being liked. In fact, the practical aspects of this ministry are not about feelings or perceptions—they are about the facts. Did we do what we said we would do? Did we plan our work and work our plan? Did we set out a list of things to do, set dates and people's names by each one and accomplish them? Did we not only work hard, but work effectively? There is a difference.

Effective work	Hard but not effective work
A short, clear description of what the money will be used for	Pages and pages of exhaustive descriptions of the good things the church has done in its history
Working hard the four weeks prior to the kick off dinner to get 90 percent attendance	Spending hours on food, decorations and set-up only to have a few members attend
Going to the top twenty wealthiest people in the church and asking them for major gifts, raising $80,000	Spending hours preparing a wordy letter to the congregation and then having the top twenty wealthiest congregants give the same average gift as the rest of the congregations, for a total of $30,000

The key to getting a job done is crafting a strong strategic plan, working hardest on the most productive tasks and being careful not to get sidetracked with things that are urgent but not, in the end, important.

Why subtract "nice" and add "kind"? To confuse "kind" and "nice" is to drink the proverbial Kool-Aid. The two must be distinguished. Nice is a form of communication that pleases people in the moment but does not relate honest feeling or truth. It often defeats the purpose of effective action. Here is what I mean in terms of fearless church fundraising:

Nice	Effective and Kind
Compliment a failed campaign	Thank someone for their hard work on the dinner but, later, review the three reasons it was a failure so that it does not happen again
Have the rector or senior pastor send out yet another rambling, self-referential letter to announce stewardship campaign season	Let the church leadership body lead a campaign that asks boldly for financial support of mission and spiritual conversion of life around money
Cave in to a contract with mediocrity and pleasantness that allows a church congregation to silence the stewardship message and fundraising management	Stand up to criticism while offering a series of events that engage all members and focus on clear teaching about money, faith, stewardship and the sins of greed, envy and lust

Nice does not have a place in genuine leadership, certainly not leadership around stewardship. On the other hand, I much prefer "kind" in church. It is kind to help people (even when those people do not want to be helped) to have a better understanding of their church and its role in the community and wider world, their money and the importance of giving it away. It is kind to help the church to thrive by raising money fearlessly and to help members to resist media and consumer culture by giving through a compelling stewardship campaign.

Nurture a Vibrant Church

I often attend worship at a church that has asked me to help them raise money. Before the offertory begins, it is often easy to see why people are not giving. The clergy seem clinically depressed. The congregation seems drugged. The music is funeral. The sermon is entirely self-focused. The ushers lack an awareness of the basics of hospitality and welcome.

These people are not greedy—they are bored and, quite possibly, spiritually depressed. Acedia has crept in.

Invariably, the fundraising in any church is going to be either hindered or helped by the effectiveness of all leadership in the church. Weak or disorganized leadership, conflict, misconduct, a lack of attention to beauty and the details of worship, poor or absent teaching and formation—all these will have a negative effect on fundraising in a church, no matter how hard the Stewardship Committee is working.

On the other hand, beautiful worship, meaningful connections within the church community, engagement with poor and marginalized people—all these work together to support fundraising, because they are the core work of the church for the glory of God.

In the past church people may not have had much choice. In the 1940s people went to their local church, regardless of if it was a good, effective, well-managed and inspiring place. It was part of the fabric of civic life, and few asked questions. Today all bets are off. People searching for a church to attend will drive past four or ten churches to get to the one they like—the one that is well-run, moving and efficient with their money.

The good news is that effective, well managed churches will thrive. The bad news is that with the speed of communication via the Internet, poorly managed churches or dull preaching may be announced on Twitter in real time. Congregants in those churches simply will withhold their pledges or find another church, leaving stagnant churches to fold one after another in the next decade.

People will pledge to and give to an agency that has asked their opinion long before it has asked for their money. Churches led by open, honest service-oriented people who lead with humility and transparency will ask members often and openly for feedback and will, in turn, encourage giving.

It is essential for the church fundraiser to discern what is going on, to be the organization's conscience and ear to the ground. The fundraising leader can then work with colleagues to make systemic change if change is needed. Fundraising is the friend of the good leader and the foe of the poor leader.

Deserve the Money

Every day, people make judgments as to what they will support based on how inspired they are by what they see and hear in a ministry. They are asking themselves these basic questions:

- Given how hard I work for the money I earn, will my money do good things if I give it to this organization?
- Given all the things in the world which need to be improved, fixed or healed, is this group's mission the most urgent and important thing to which I should be giving?
- Does this organization fit with what I consider to be the most essential work of goodness in the world?
- Am I (or can I imagine being) physically involved in this work? Can my body be involved in what my money is doing to heal the world?
- Have they told a story to me that is as compelling or more compelling than the story my school, university, hospital, YMCA, United Way and local museum have told me?

It may be true that faith-based organizations still receive the largest proportion of giving in America. That does not mean churches will automatically receive or should assume they deserve that giving.

In fact, God only says in scripture we are to give to the poor and the marginalized. God does not say that we need to give to the church. We need to give to God through the church if the particular church in question deserves the money and will use it well. The good news (or the bad news) is that God is indeed bringing the kingdom into existence, but only occasionally is God using the church.

Later, we will go into more detail about how to tell your story when fundraising in the church. Fundraisers call it case development. For now, know that your ability to raise money depends, today, on how you tell the story and prove you deserve what people have worked so hard to earn.

The church fundraiser is not only gathering money for the church to run. He or she has a unique opportunity to help foster a stronger congregation that exhibits effective, kind leadership; maintains a robust spiritual and organizational life; and can prove it is worth the people's investment because it is participating in God's mission.

Having committed to that work, the ministry can then take the practical steps ahead in order to raise money and raise it well.

## CHAPTER 5

Stewardship Campaign Leadership

The word "campaign" comes from the late Middle Ages, the days of villages and castles. To organize an effort like a battle, lots of people had to leave the safety of their individual hovels and gather on an open field. They were organized into lines and columns in order to move forward together, under strong leadership. This is the way towns and villages have worked for hundreds of years: gather, organize, give a leader authority to lead.

My use of the word "ministry" here is also not an accident. This is not only a Pledge Campaign, not simply quick-fix work done in haste in August and September. It is a ministry. Prayer and regular spiritual practice should already be or should soon become a primary part of the campaign and the leaders' lives, so that they can model discernment, integrity, maturity and spiritual centeredness to the rest of the congregation.

Roles of Campaign Leadership

The finances of a church are too important to leave to chance. People's jobs, ministries and some lives may even be on the line if budgets crash due to failed stewardship campaigns or lackluster fundraising.

For this reason, leadership should not be left to those who volunteer for positions. These jobs require effective leadership and the ramifications of not getting the job done can be debilitating. This is not a time to ask for hands at a vestry meeting. Regardless of whether you have a congregation of thirty or three thousand, the clergy and lay leaders' co-creative task is to look closely at the human resources in the congregation and make strategic, clear requests for the help needed.

Each job done by a key leader or volunteer in the campaign needs a job description with clearly defined, measurable tasks, as well as clear term limits. These may be based on the descriptions below.

In a small church with few leaders available, simply choose one person who is known to get a job done and relieve them of other responsibilities while they are planning and managing the campaign. The best leaders are the busy ones. Less effective leaders are usually very available with little on their calendar. For key positions choose people who have a reputation for honesty and for getting jobs done when and as they said they would.

Like it or not, inside and outside the church, donors are to some extent investing based on their confidence in the leadership. That is why, when there is a change in leadership, giving can slip if advance communications systems have not planned for the vulnerability of change. As long as the people making the pledge are confident of the leadership (even temporary leadership) then their giving will not be eroded by change.

Here are some of the key roles and descriptions of each leadership role in relationship to stewardship, with the Episcopal Church as my guide (though these categories can be adapted for other faith communities' structures):

The bishop is responsible for the ministry of the diocese and the care of the clergy. Part of this responsibility is for finances that make programs and ministries possible. The stewardship of the people of the diocese as well as the stewardship of diocesan funds is of utmost importance to the bishop. The bishop is responsible for putting staff and systems in place to assist the diocese with the important and life-giving work of raising money for the ministry of the diocese.

The bishop should personally speak to each parochial clergy person to relay his or her expectations regarding the work of annual, capital, major gift and planned giving work in that congregation, and to highlight diocesan opportunities for training and wider-church stewardship services.

In some cases, such as a diocesan capital campaign, the bishop may work with staff and local clergy to ask for major gifts from very wealthy people whose gift can be combined to benefit both their local church and the larger diocese or Episcopal Church, but this kind of "cherry-picking" of major diocesan donors needs to be done very carefully so as not to alienate the clergy from their bishop in the event that the bishop is perceived as taking gifts that could otherwise have benefitted a local parish.

The top 5 percent of donors in any diocese have the capacity to make gifts much larger than their local church could possibly use well, but in that event, the gift needs to be asked for carefully, and with open dialogue between the bishop and local lay and clerical leadership.

The canon to the ordinary is usually the bishop's chief of staff and often works on deployment of clergy. This leader should be in constant communication with the bishop and other diocesan leaders to raise their awareness of clergy and lay leaders whose life or work situation may have an effect on stewardship planning or implementation. As clergy are being recruited to a diocese, a Canon to the Ordinary might look for clergy with proven skill and success in financial development and stewardship campaign management and implementation.

The canon or director for stewardship, development, congregational life or congregational development provides resources that help the clergy and lay leaders to manage the spiritual and logistical details of congregational life. Stewardship support should be part of this leaders' whole toolbox, treated alongside vitality assessment and training, asset mapping, communications, strategic planning, mutual ministry reviews and ministry development. Sadly, many denominations and dioceses do not employ people to assist churches with fundraising—usually because they cannot afford to pay someone, an ironic and unfortunate decision.

The rector (or vicar, priest-in-charge, pastor, minister, shepherd) is responsible for knowing and loving the people in his or her parish enough to help them boldly engage the difficult conversation about faith and money. The rector needs to strive towards the biblical tithe as a model of right relationship with money and God. The rector should also be familiar with the bounty or scarcity, gifts and needs, in the lives of parishioners—be they financial, relational or spiritual.

The rector is responsible for assembling a budget infused with resources necessary for profound ministry to occur, and that includes the responsibility to ensure sufficient funds are raised for ministry. The rector *should not* be made responsible for a budget and at the same time remain blind to the resources that fund that budget.

Though it can be a touchy subject, it is best for the rector to know what people pledge and whether people pay their pledge. The rector need not worry that having this information will affect his or her relationship with members. Just as hearing confessions should not change a priest-parishioner relationship, neither should knowledge of pledge amounts change the pastoral relationship.

The wardens or chief lay leaders function in much the same way that a chairman of a board of directors works with the executive director of a corporation or nonprofit. The wardens hold the primary responsibility for ensuring that the members fund a budget that supports vibrant and courageous ministry, and that the ministry is worthy of the gifts pledged. Like the rector, the wardens should strive toward the biblical tithe as a model of right relationship with money and God.

Clergy will come and clergy will go. The church is made up of the people, and the people must take the responsibility for funding their own mission. It is the responsibility of the wardens to make this happen and the responsibility of the clergy to see to it that the vestry and wardens have adequate support to do their job.

The vestry or bishop's committee or church council is responsible for pledging with boldness so as to set a true leading example. The vestry should make their pledges early (along with the staff) and may publicly walk their pledge commitment cards to the altar as a symbol to the congregation that they are leading by example.

Vestry members who do not pledge should be invited clearly and firmly to find other lay ministries within the church. They need not tithe, because some truly cannot spare 10 percent of their income while others will not be challenged enough by a 10-percent gift. The pledge could be 5 percent or 50 percent; the point is to make a plan to contribute a portion of one's income.

The stewardship or pledge campaign ministry chairperson guides development of a strategic, detailed, working plan for the stewardship campaign. The chair must find creative ways to articulate why the money is needed and why it should be pledged (this is called the "case for support").

Ideally, a Stewardship Ministry has a chairperson and a rising chair (the leader-in-training). The rising chair can then be moved to chair every three years. The idea is that there is always someone in the wings ready to assess the work (in case the chair begins to drop the ball), while the chair is always training someone else so that there is no threat of a leadership vacuum.

The stewardship or pledge campaign ministry leaders manage the strategic plan of the Stewardship Pledge Campaign. Ministry leaders should meet year-round, reporting in writing to the vestry monthly with their status on their strategic plan from January until the beginning of the active campaign. When the campaign begins, they should shift to meeting weekly to analyze the campaign's status and make adjustments for momentum and effectiveness. Each chair and committee member should have a written job description with a term limit not to exceed six years.

Administrative or secretarial staff (if you have one) supports the wardens, vestry and Stewardship Ministry in their work. Remember that there is considerable clerical work involved in effective fundraising, largely because there is a lot of communication. Here is a list of some of the tasks that will need to be managed in even a small campaign:

- All-parish letters and e-mails
- Web info about pledging
- Special event (Kickoff and Victory Celebrations) invitations, notices and reminders
- Production of weekly mailers with campaign status—this can be done months in advance with five or six different templates set up and then simply filled in with weekly statistics on campaign status, printed, labeled and mailed (or e-mailed)
- Pledge cards
- Non-pick-up pledge card cover letter and mailing
- Campaign case brochure or mailing
- Thank-you letters for tax purposes (may be done by treasurer)
- Campaign files for management and evaluation and for archive
- Bulletin inserts and ministry minutes
- Phone-a-thons for campaign closure

Consider sending your parish secretary or your campaign chairperson a gift at the beginning, acknowledging all the work the campaign will involve and then a second gift when the campaign is complete. It takes money to make money—even in the nonprofit and ecclesial sectors. If you are raising $50,000 then you can certainly spend $50 to thank the person whose hard work made it all possible—especially if you want them to do it again next year!

Remember that much of the resistance discussed in the early chapters of this book will be directed at clerical staff and lay-volunteer leadership. Be sensitive to the impact of that resistance, and take good care of those who are working hard for the campaign's success.

Stewardship Leaders' Ideal Qualifications

Chair of Stewardship Ministry

This is a very important choice. For the record, in my experience, co-chairs are far less effective. The buck needs to stop somewhere. The following are key aspects of a strong candidate:

- An able person with proven leadership skills who attends worship regularly and embodies prayer, love and balance
- A person who makes generous and consistent financial contributions to the parish, who pledges a percentage of his or her income and who maintains a standard of living in keeping with the gospel
- A person who is well known to and trusted by the congregation and who both likes and has a good relationship with the clergy and vestry
- A person who does what they say they will do and has a track record to prove it
- A person committed to success, enough that they could pull a struggling campaign over the finish line
- A person with enthusiasm for the mission of the church and of the parish, enough to meet the most difficult challenges and resistance of other parishioners
- A person who is generous with his or her time, understanding that campaigns usually require dozens of meetings: vestry, committee, coaching meetings, kickoffs, events, announcements in church, strategic planning sessions, etc.

Stewardship Campaign Chair Job Description

- Receives campaign recommendations from vestry, clergy and staff, works with the clergy on revisions, and approves recommendations
- Recruits and supervises campaign volunteers including event planners, pledge accountants, communications management, etc.
- Plans kickoff and campaign close celebrations
- Works on major gift requests, including directly asking for gifts (with clergy support where needed)
- Manages resistance within congregation
- Evaluates the Annual Pledge Campaign: What went well? What did not go well? What would one change next year? (three questions that ideally follow every event and program)

- Prays for and witnesses to a vibrant and healthy relationship with money and God
- Engages in discernment about his or her household's pledge and makes a pledge that represents a financial challenge

The Clergy Leader Job Description

The clergy leader is responsible for the day-to-day execution of the Annual Pledge Campaign effort, unless other staff or leaders have been designated. Clergy are responsible for managing stewardship programs (raising the money) because they are responsible for budgets (managing and spending the money).

In the most effective campaigns I have seen, the clergy leader partners closely with the campaign chairperson and directs the campaign by performing the following tasks:

- Prepares the General Strategic Plan draft (containing the campaign goal, table of organization, important campaign strategies, campaign calendar, expense budget, job descriptions, etc.); all tasks should have a deadline and the name of the person responsible for completion of the task
- Prepares the campaign case draft detailing the money needed to fulfill the congregation's mission in the next year
- Works as staff liaison to the vestry around the Stewardship Ministry
- Serves as the congregation's chief spiritual and logistical planner, resource and campaign expert
- Supports the Stewardship Ministry Chair in recruiting the campaign committee members
- Prevents lay leadership from undertaking unproductive stewardship campaign practices or getting side-tracked on urgent but unimportant activities
- Organizes the stewardship campaign systems to provide accurate records and controls: master lists, campaign records, mailings, auditing and reporting systems
- Protects and produces prospect lists for all levels of major gift requests
- Coordinates training and motivational efforts throughout the campaign, including preaching, teaching and making or coaching motivational announcements
- Reports accurate and timely results to ensure all lay leaders are up to date on the campaign's progress
- Ensures that all pledgers and volunteers are acknowledged and thanked for their efforts and sacrifice

- Exerts strong personal leadership on the total organization and effort

As the church changes to reflect increased lay leadership and decreased dependence on full-time clergy, these tasks may be outsourced. That shift may release the clergy to do the teaching and formation which undergirds the fundraising effort.

The only warning is that clergy must be responsible for outcomes. The clergy leader must consider the campaign of highest priority, influencing vestry members, committee members and other lay leaders to assure successful formation, engagement and fundraising. Success in stewardship needs to be a central aspect of the regular job performance evaluation or mutual ministry review performed by laity. Without that commitment accountability, the campaign will fail, no matter how competent the staff, vestry, committee members and lay leadership.

The Vestry Role in Stewardship

The role of lay (non-clergy) leadership in stewardship planning and management cannot be underestimated. It is the people's church, and so it is the people's responsibility to raise the money needed to be the church. Too often vestries grow uncomfortable talking about money, so they outsource the entire campaign to a Stewardship Committee, celebrating success with them if the campaign succeeds or possibly scapegoating them if the campaign fails.

In the event that yours is a small church with few leaders, the vestry member best suited to stewardship leadership may sit on the vestry and manage stewardship planning and management at the same time (and everything else for that matter!).

The following are some of the key responsibilities of the vestry or church leadership throughout the year:

- Discern mission, work with clergy to craft a budget that reflects the mission with the input and involvement of the congregation and raise funds through Stewardship Ministry to enable mission
- Request and hear a written and spoken report from the Stewardship Chairperson each month throughout the year. During campaign season, the reports will be focused on status; the rest of the year, the report will be focused on planning or evaluation.
- Read and discuss the revised stewardship strategic plan—a full-year plan—as presented by the Stewardship Ministry
- Develop and review members' relationship to and involvement with the church

- At least two weeks prior to the Kickoff Celebration, vestry members do need to pray about and make their pledges in writing. We suggest the vestry consider a public announcement of their support in the context of worship such as a procession of pledge cards to the altar. The congregation needs to see and know that the vestry has modeled good stewardship and are invested.
- Review strategic plans monthly and ensure with clergy and campaign leadership that plans are executed on schedule
- Pray regularly for the congregation and assist the clergy leader in reviewing member lists to determine better and more effective ways to involve each congregant in the life and ministry of the church. Members have to be more than passive observers of liturgies if they are to become passionate donors to the program and ministry of the church.
- Attend all key events of the campaign, especially the Kickoff and Victory Celebrations. Vestry attendance at all key leadership opportunities is essential.

All these leaders, together, can spur a ministry that enhances connection and engagement, all of which, in turn, lead to robust giving . . . and conversion of lives around money and giving.

## CHAPTER 6

Weaving Stewardship Formation into Church Life

Five minutes a day with a lit candle or a silent walk in the woods in listening prayer with God will, I am convinced, change the world and transform stewardship. In that discipline and rule of life, the Holy Spirit will convert souls from fear to gratitude and from greed to giving.

Clergy and laity in large and small churches might ask some of the following questions as they plan their work and ministry in tending to the spiritual lives of their congregants:

- What in our worship teaches the fundamentals of giving?
- What fears around money, giving and standards of living exist in our church culture?
- Has there been any misconduct or conflict that needs to be addressed and healed, lest it erode giving?
- What hymns do we sing, and which ones speak to fearlessness, gratitude, sharing and generosity?
- What rotation of prayers and collects can we use each Sunday to form the congregation and to beg God's assistance in this work of helping people to give?
- When and how often are we hosting compelling, creative and informative conversations around money and giving? Has our congregation been given the opportunity to consider where fear and money overlap in their history, family, life experience and world-view?
- What is the strategic plan for ministry in this place? Do people know what we are spending money and time on and are they willing to invest in that mission?

- What teaching is specifically being done around the following areas:
  — Rule of Life
  — Family financial planning
  — Mission and ministry
  — Fear and theodicy (explanation of how or why God allows evil)
  — Giving and pledging
  — Church finances
  — Membership
  — Sacrifice and counter-cultural living
  — Prayer and meditation

Every congregation needs regular, careful teaching and formation on these issues, so that pledging rests in the context of a larger understanding of church membership, Christian identity and stewardship of resources. This chapter features examples and models of formation resources for adults and young people. For copies of these samples, as well as video and other resources, please go to www.churchpublishing.org/fearlesschurchfundraising.

Adult Forums on Money

How We Deal with Our Money as Christians

(One 60-minute session or three 20-minute sessions)

Using the Introduction and Part I of the book *Fearless Church Fundraising* as a guide, the facilitator leads discussion on these questions:

1. What blocks our giving?

   a. Fear and the effects of the media

   b. Fear of poverty

   c. Fear of abandonment and vulnerability

   d. Need for financial security versus faith

   e. Exhaustion and over-stimulation

   f. Telling our story of where and when money and fear met in our lives

2. Some have said human beings are made good by God and streaked with evil, rather than made evil and streaked with good. How does this understanding of human nature change the way we see God, ourselves and our money?

   a. God's creation of the world as "very good"

   b. The incarnation of Christ as God honoring creation and worldly things

   c. Describe childhood views of God: angry schoolmaster? disappointed parent?

   d. Describe mature views of God: extravagant giver of all good things? model of sacrificial giving?

   e. Describe childhood views of money: filthy lucre? root of evil?

   f. Describe mature views of money: a tool for good? grows as shared?

3. Why do we give as part of our relationship with God?

   a. Covenant: God makes covenant with humanity, we make covenants with each other

   b. What we are not doing: tipping God, paying for services enjoyed or rendered

   c. Impact of giving to God on relationship with God (versus impact of withholding)

4. How does giving to our church impact others' lives? Why have an Annual Stewardship Campaign?

   a. Impact of giving on relationship with community (versus withholding)

   b. What human needs in our community does giving address?

   c. Discuss concept of church "deserving" the money it raises

   d. Notice relationship of salaries and buildings to ministry and pastoral care

5. How can stewardship be a theological, spiritual practice and not merely a logistical one?

   a. Giving as part of a Rule of Life guiding use of time, talent, treasure

   b. Practice giving one day at a time, like regular prayer, setting goals and slowly increasing your capacity and generosity

   c. Reconciliation and right relationship with God and each other

Family Reflection on Money, Giving and God

The best way for people to become good stewards of their money and to learn good habits of giving is in the home, modeled by parents. These resources are written to help a family work together to consider their pledge, to teach the importance of pledging to the ministries of the church, and to grasp the importance of giving back to God a portion of that which is God's.

Opening Prayer: A Collect for Stewardship

Gracious God, giver of all we have and hold; grant the people of this church a deep and abiding awareness that all things come from you—our health, our incomes, our jobs, our talents, and our generous impulses. Send your Holy Spirit to help us as we swim against the rising tides of materialism, envy, individualism and greed in our culture. When we are tempted to think of money as a private matter, remind us that you have asked for part of what we are given, to be returned to you as a symbol of our awareness that you give all we have. And finally, assist us as we help each other to embrace the grace of giving, for you are the lover of our souls and call us to nothing less than transformation in Jesus Christ our Lord. AMEN.

For Group or Individual Reflection:

1. What is our personal and family relationship with money?

2. How do we, as a family, talk about money?

3. In what ways do our relationship with God and money intersect?

4. What fears do we have around money?

5. When was the first time fear and money intersected in our individual lives or our family life? What happened? What fears about money do we now live with, as a result?

6. What is our church's relationship with money?

7. How do we talk about money as a congregation?

8. What happens if we do not pledge? If we do?

9. What does the church do with the money we pledge?

■■■

Tips on Speaking to Young People about Pledging

Many parents find that the most effective way to teach stewardship and pledging is to provide children with a means by which to earn money and then discuss the setting aside of some of that money for the pledge.

Churches can help by providing color-coded pledge cards for children, along with the family pledge cards given out at the start of a campaign. This pledge card can begin the conversation with children about giving.

Consider weekly payment of pledges rather than one-time gifts, so that the connection between income and outflow of pledge is clear. It is also valuable for children to visit outreach sites and see other functions of the church up close so they can see the work their pledge has enabled.

Whatever your Sunday School and formation plans, be sure that all curricula include responsible discussion of stewardship. Many resources are available for teaching young people about possessions, money, giving and fear, including the basic sketch provided in this book (to be adapted with age-appropriate supplementary materials).

Six-week Sunday School Lesson on Stewardship

1. **Jesus and Money**: Read the story of the Rich Young Ruler (Matthew 19:16–26 or Luke 18:18–23). Have the children act out or in some other way portray the various scenes in this passage. Then discuss these questions:

   a. Why is Jesus cranky with this man?

   b. What is the man asking for?

   c. What is the man afraid of?

   d. How does the story end in the passage?

   e. What might the man do or experience after he leaves Jesus?

2. **Media and Consumerism**: Show several television or magazine advertisements that use fear, body image or envy to sell a product. Lead the children in discussing what they saw and why making careful choices about money and spending is so important.

   a. What insecurities did the ad encourage?

   b. Why might a person want to make this purchase? Why not?

   c. Why and how does what we "see" affect our sense of self? How does what we see affect our relationship to God?

3. **God's Bounty**: Lay out a banquet for the kids and ask them to discuss bounty.

   a. What are the gardens in scripture (Eden, Songs, Gethsemane, Resurrection, Revelation)? Why are there so many? What do they seem to represent?

   b. Farmers in scripture left the edges of their crops for the poor (Deuteronomy 24:19–21). Why do you think they engaged in that practice? How could we do something similar today, though we are not farmers?

   c. Our planet is designed to support life for eight billion people. It only feeds three billion of the existing six billion well. Why are so many hungry in a world of plenty?

   d. What does it mean to give God some of our money through the church? How can we help God to provide for others?

4. **Scarcity**: Consider the two versions of the Beatitudes, especially the references to "poverty of spirit" (Matthew 5:3) and to "the poor" (Luke 6:20). Then ask the children:

   a. Have you ever felt you did not have enough for yourself to give some away? Tell the story. How did it feel?

   b. Has someone ever given you something and you knew it was a sacrifice? Tell the story. How did it feel?

   c. Have you ever given something to another person even though it felt like a sacrifice for you? Tell the story. How did it feel?

   d. What does it mean to "live simply so that others may simply live"?

   e. What is the difference between quantity and quality? Why might one great bite of a beloved fruit be better than a huge buffet of bland food?

5. **Gratitude**: Consider with the youth what gratitude is and why it is important to giving.

   a. Name one thing today for which you are grateful.

   b. Name one thing today for which you are unable to be grateful.

   c. What does it mean for God to be the one who gives us all that we have?

   d. Talk about a time in your life when you shared something with someone else. What did it feel like? Where in your body is that feeling, if you had to choose a place?

   e. How could you show gratitude to God for all that you have? How do we do that in church?

6. **Philanthropy**: Philanthropy simply describes the things we do to show that we love other human beings, especially giving some of our money to help those who need our help.

   a. How does our church use the money we give?

   b. What does our church do in the community to help people who are hurting?

   c. What does our church do inside the congregation to help us when we are suffering?

   d. Why is it important to help those around us who need help?

   e. Have you ever given something away that was important to you or valuable? What did it feel like?

Financial Planning as Spiritual Practice
A Three-part Adult Formation Program

Session 1: Hope and fear around money and giving

1. Your hopes around money

   a. What are your hopes for financial freedom?

   b. What do you sense the church has to do or say about financial freedom in your household?

   c. What does Jesus mean when he refers to wanting us to have life "abundant"?

   d. Jesus said, more than anything else, "Do not be afraid!" Why was this?

   e. How does money inspire fear in our culture?

   f. Around what do you feel fear?

   g. Where is there fear in the media?

   h. Why raise such a private matter as personal finance in church or in the family?

2. Your fear around money

   Reflect on these biblical passages. What words stand out to you? What passage resonates most for you? What does it inspire you to do about your fear? What do these words tell you about the reality of fear in spiritual life?

   a. "People will faint from fear and foreboding of what is coming upon the world, for the powers of the heavens will be shaken." Luke 21:26

   b. "The thief comes only to steal and kill and destroy. I came that they may have life, and have it abundantly." John 10:10

   c. "There they shall be in great terror, in terror such as has not been." Psalm 53:5

3. Media and fear

Reflect on these facts around the media, fear and money. How does our intake of this information affect the way we spend and the way we live?

a. Number of murders seen on TV by the time an average child finishes elementary school: 8,000

b. Number of violent acts seen on TV by age 18: 200,000

c. Number of 30-second TV commercials seen in a year by an average child: 20,000

d. Number of TV commercials seen by the average person by age 65: 2 million[5]

4. Your story of fear and money

Form pairs and tell the story of the first time in your life that fear and money coincided. When did you first become afraid about some aspect of money? What did it feel like? Where in your body did you feel the fear? How did that fear influence your life and your choices? How does it now?

5. Your family and money

In pairs, tell the story of how your family talked about or avoided talking about money. How does that pattern affect you and your feelings about money today?

---

5. Figures from A.C. Nielsen Co. http://www.csun.edu/science/health/docs/tv&health.html

Financial Planning as Spiritual Practice
A Three-part Adult Formation Program

Session 2: A Rule of Life Chapter on Money

Introduction to a Rule of Life

A "Rule of Life" sounds like a daunting thing. "Rule": the word itself can feel confining, imprisoning. It quickly conjures images of frustrated nuns with rulers ready to rap your knuckles if you step out of line. Our society highly values open options and places a very low value on commitment. Playing by the rules is downright un-American.

And yet, our choices matter. When we choose one thing—having done the hard work of discerning that which is right and best for us, in this moment—we must release the many other possibilities we did not choose.

Making a choice and living it out well is hard work, is limiting and is a sign of spiritual and emotional maturity. A Rule of Life is one of many tools employed for centuries to channel our natural, human, God-given passions much the way a garden hose nozzle will focus a wide, gentle spray of water over a garden into a powerful stream of water which can take paint off the side of a house. A Rule of Life is not meant to *deny* as much as it is meant to *focus* power, naturally limited resources of time, energy, money, emotional investment and passion into a life lived abundantly rather than simply largely.

A Rule of Life helps me to define what I want from my life and to discern what is in line with God's hope for my life. It also serves as a reminder or a guardrail, reminding me of God's hopes and my intentions, so that my wanderings do not take me too far off the path.

Writing a Chapter of Your Rule of Life on Money

Individual or Group Exercise: Have each person write a chapter for their rule of life on the subject of money, possessions, giving, pledging, stewardship or simplicity.

Step 1: Do a search of scripture by word or phrase to find passages that apply to this subject. Here is a sampling:

For which of you, intending to build a tower, does not first sit down and estimate the cost, to see whether he has enough to complete it? Otherwise, when he has laid a foundation and is not able to finish, all who see it will begin to ridicule him, saying, "This fellow began to build and was not able to finish." (Luke 14:28–30)

Therefore do not worry, saying, "What will we eat?" or "What will we drink?" or "What will we wear?" For it is the Gentiles who strive for all these things; and indeed your heavenly Father knows that you need all these things. But strive first for the kingdom of God and his righteousness, and all these things will be given to you as well. (Matthew 6:31–33)

I have learned to be content with whatever I have. I know what it is to have little, and I know what it is to have plenty. In any and all circumstances I have learned the secret of being well-fed and of going hungry, of having plenty and of being in need. I can do all things through him who strengthens me. (Philippians 4:11b–13)

We brought nothing into the world, so that we can take nothing out of it; but if we have food and clothing, we will be content with these. But those who want to be rich fall into temptation and are trapped by many senseless and harmful desires that plunge people into ruin and destruction. For the love of money is a root of all kinds of evil, and in their eagerness to be rich some have wandered away from the faith and pierced themselves with many pains. (1 Timothy 6:7–10)

Keep your lives free from the love of money, and be content with what you have; for he has said, "I will never leave you or forsake you." (Hebrews 13:5)

The LORD will open for you his rich storehouse, the heavens, to give the rain of your land in its season and to bless all your undertakings. You will lend to many nations, but you will not borrow. (Deuteronomy 28:12)

The rich rule over the poor,
and the borrower is the slave of the lender. (Proverbs 22:7)

All shall give as they are able, according to the blessing of the LORD your God that he has given you. (Deuteronomy 16:17)

Do not withhold good from those to whom it is due,
when it is in your power to do it. (Proverbs 3:27)

[Jesus] said to them, "Whoever has two coats must share with anyone who has none; and whoever has food must do likewise." (Luke 3:11)

Step 2: Meditate on these or other money-related passages. Pray them. Think on them. Be in conversation with others about them.

Step 3: Outline the chapter, using brief sentence fragments. This outline works for nearly any topic, and you can fill it with your own content regarding money:

- Theology of the topic
- Spirituality of the topic
- The practical realities of the topic for my life
- The desire I have to make this topic happen in my spiritual life
- Why I consider this topic to be important for my conversion
- My hopes for how God will assist and provide for me in this topic

Step 4: When your preparation is complete, start writing your chapter. Be clear and simple, not too wordy, and use short sentences where possible. I find that five hundred words—one page single-spaced— is the most you want in a chapter.

Step 5: Finish and begin to live it out, remembering that each chapter is a work in progress until death. Be open to making changes. Keep wide margins so that you can make notes about changes as you use the rule.

Sample Chapter of a Rule of Life

The Stewardship of Money

My heart tells me that all shall be well, that everything I have comes from God and that I have enough. The media tells me that my money is a way to get what I want and that I do not have enough. Our "work" is not to believe the stories in our heads, regardless of who or what put them there and especially if they have been placed there by the media. Our story of "not enough" . . . "need more" . . . "I will be poor" . . . "my money will protect me" . . . these are all just our thoughts. Our work is not to believe everything we think.

I am aware that I have been raised by people whose attachment to money was not healthy and I seek healing in the area of money. I am also aware that occasionally I will attempt to soothe hurt feelings, insecurities, loneliness or boredom by spending money, both in an effort to establish power and control, and also as a means to purchase things that give me a momentary sense of satisfaction.

As I look at the life of Jesus, I see a man who lived with what he had and with what was given to him. That is my hope for my life as well. I desire to ask myself—every time I spend money—if I really need what I am buying.

My hope is that I will live simply, that I will be aware and attentive to what I have and what I spend and that I will live on or work towards living on 80 percent of my income while saving 20 percent of my income.

My hope is that I will live within my means on a weekly basis, never misusing credit by purchasing unessential things for which I do not have the funds available. I will allow myself to feel the poverty of having to say "no" to myself when I want something I cannot afford. I will live by a budget, checking my progress regularly so as not to overspend. I will be attentive to turning off lights, taking care with food leftovers and using firewood, so as not to waste what God has given to me.

It will be my goal to offer gratitude for what I have when I awake before getting out of bed, and when I lay down before I sleep, listing in the context of a prayer what I have been given.

My gifts to the church and to myself through my savings will always be the first checks I write each month. I will set aside four hours twice a month to manage my finances. My home and related expenses will not exceed 30 percent of my income regardless of how simply I must live, in order to maintain a level of financial freedom, security and generosity. I will seek help when I find myself wanting to "keep up with the Joneses" (or the Kardashians).

And when I wish I had more than I have, I will try to remember how much I *do* have, and squeeze out a prayer of gratitude as an antidote to envy or despair.

■ ■

Financial Planning as Spiritual Practice
A Three-part Adult Formation Program

Session 3: Money Management as Spiritual Practice

Opening Exercise:

Discuss in pairs your short-term goals concerning your personal finances. Then write the goals and share them with the group to build community and accountability.

Five Elements of Financial Fitness:

1. **Limited Short-Term Debt**

   a. Cut up your credit cards as it becomes possible

   b. Fix credit scores through disciplined payment of debts and budgeting

   c. Enjoy the freedom of living with integrity between what you believe and what you do, and be released from fear and shame that accompany indebtedness

2. **Adequate Liquidity**

   a. Have a savings cushion of four to six months of daily living expenses on hand in liquid form (i.e., if you make $30,000 and live on that much money, then you should have $12,000 as a minimum in savings)

   b. If using a retirement account to save, choose the most liquid form, rather than one that is severely penalized if withdrawn prior to retirement

3. **Adequate Savings**

   a. If you have created a realistic budget and live within your means, you will likely have excess money to set aside, money that now works for you

b. Aim to save 10 percent of your income as permanent savings for use in retirement. In thirty-five years, if you begin saving at this rate at age twenty-five, you could live off your savings

c. Add the 10 percent of personal savings to the savings plan offered by your employer

4. **Own a right-sized house:**

a. Try to put 20 percent down as the initial deposit in order to keep interest rates lower

b. Remember that a mortgaged house is the best hedge against inflation

c. Remember that mortgage interest and property tax are deductible

d. How much house should you buy? The general rule is two to three-and-a-half times your income. If you make $45,000, you could buy a home valued at $100,000 to $175,000.

Prayers for Stewardship

It amazes me that we do not pray more about money in church. Generally, this liturgical reticence to discuss money with God, out loud, can be traced to demands that we keep "the holy" and "the worldly" separate. And yet, when we are burying a loved one, we pray for consolation. When we are in a disaster, our Great Litany invites us to pray for help. When we ordain and baptize, we pray for wisdom and strength.

Why, when we are raising money for a mission God clearly desires in this world, are we hesitant to ask for changed hearts, reduced fears, soothed longings, awareness of bounty, gratitude for blessings and strength to give our money away?

In liturgy, the people need to hear and offer prayers that help them with the internal work to release their death-grip on money. If we sanitize our prayers of all references to our need for money, we are teaching the congregation to hide part of their lives from God.

Prayer for a Faithful Relationship with Money

Gracious God, giver of all we have and hold; grant the people of this church a deep and abiding awareness that all things come from you— our health, our incomes, our jobs, our talents and our generous impulse. Send your Holy Spirit to help us as we swim against the rising tides of materialism, envy, individualism and greed in our culture. When we are tempted to think of money as a private matter, remind us that you have asked for part of what we are given, to be returned to you as a symbol of our awareness that you give all we have. And finally, assist us as we help each other to embrace the grace of giving, for you are the lover of our souls and call us to nothing less than transformation in Jesus Christ our Lord. AMEN.

Prayer for the Provision of Finances

Blessed are you, Lord God of the Universe, for you create out of the cosmos this fragile earth and give life to it. You maintain our lives with the spark of our heartbeat and the growth of food from the earth. How can we do anything but respond by giving back a portion of our blessings to the life and ministry of the church, your body on earth? Help us to be less afraid of vulnerability and thereby to loosen our death-grip on our money. Help us to see clearly the inequality in our world and to respond by giving through your body, the church. AMEN.

Prayer for the Provision of Time and Talent

Father, you breathed life into humanity and gave us various gifts and talents by which to live and move and have our being. Forgive us when we fall into the temptation of thinking that time and talent are made by us. Help us to see that our salaries and our hard work come only because of your provision of life and health and creativity. Help us as we struggle against a culture in which "time is money." Help us to give ourselves as you did, even unto the cross. May your self-offering be our model and may your love be our encouragement. AMEN.

Prayer for the Provision of Funds for a Capital Campaign

Lord Christ, you built the church by uniting your mother, Mary, and your disciple John at the cross. Ever since, you have encouraged the church as your body on earth to flourish and grow. From a mud hut in an ancient Celtic village to a cathedral in a bustling city, you have fed the church with energy to build and grow. As we build our church, help us to see this building as a symbol and tool for preaching the good news and living the joy of community together. Provide, through your Holy Spirit, the resources and wisdom we will need. Then, when the last stone is laid and the last board nailed, dwell with us that we might be with you and through you with each other as you are within and among the Trinity, world without end. AMEN.

Prayer for Those Leading Stewardship Ministries

Lord Christ, you held your ground as you communicated a message amidst support and amidst rejection. Give to us who lead stewardship ministries the strength to help our church to discuss that which it would rather ignore. Help us to speak openly about money, time and land as gift. Help us to respond to a culture for whom greed is nothing more than a scream of fear, so that our work might be not merely fundraising, but rather a pastoral ministry to a people weighed down by a spiritually deadly combination of abundance and fear. AMEN.

Prayer for Use by a Vestry Regarding Stewardship

Heavenly Father and Creator of all that we enjoy, we give you thanks for the countless people who have gone before us in the leadership of this church. We know that the Holy Spirit inspired some as they longed for this church, others as they built this church and still others as they lovingly and boldly led this church through times of abundance and times of scarcity. Help us to be courageous as we model giving of time and money to this parish. Make our bold and generous pledge a symbol of both our integrity and our gratitude. Then help us to encourage giving with all that we do and say, just as you did while physically teaching among your disciples. AMEN.

Prayer for Use by Children Regarding Stewardship

Jesus, we love you and we know that you love us. Everything we have is a gift from you. Thank you for play time and for our growing bodies. Thank you for our laughter and our joy. Help us to give some of our time and some of our money back to you. When we think of giving something away to someone who needs it, help us to give two and not just one. AMEN.

Preaching Stewardship and Giving

Preaching about stewardship, pledging and giving requires great care. Technically, preachers have a captive audience; people are there to worship, and the sermon is part of that worship. Walking out is technically an option, but most people would never make such a move.

A skillful preacher can be inspiring, and the same skill can be used to manipulate. It is good to know the difference. The responsible, centered, well-prayed preacher is not discouraged from preaching a strong stewardship sermon; you are cautioned to do so carefully. It is easy for your own anxiety, shame, grief and regret about money to get projected into a sermon that ends up being scolding and hollow.

I suggest spiritual-life preaching and teaching, formation and encouragement year-round. If the clergy and laity are doing that work well, then the stewardship sermon ends up being best preached by the Holy Spirit. The moving "Ministry Minutes" that members offer to share why they love this church so much, the joy of a fun campaign kickoff, the power of a bulletin insert about how a life was changed by the outreach ministry, the beauty of the silence after a great hymn—these preach stewardship better than any crafty sermon.

That said, a good preacher looks at the scripture readings to determine its focus and trajectory in the context of the life of the parish. If the text and context call for it, he or she could preach about some aspect of giving, ownership, sacrifice, envy, greed, generosity or gratitude. Just remember that, no matter how good the sermon, the congregation must deeply and fully experience the preacher as a pastor long *before* they will accept the preacher's ministry as a prophet or leader. The issue is not, "Has this preacher preached a moving stewardship sermon?" The issue is, "Does this preacher love us deeply, lead us powerfully and teach us to give our whole lives away regularly?" The second question is, "Is what we are supporting worthy of the financial sacrifice we are making? Is this the best use of my giving?"

A stewardship sermon and formation program that help to answer those two questions in the affirmative will go a long way toward advancing the campaign . . . and the kingdom of God.

....

## PART III

The Warm-up: Planning, Recruitment and Communications

CHAPTER 7

....

Prepare for Planning

Scripture says that where there is no vision, the people perish (Proverbs 29:18). To avoid effective strategic planning—especially by implying that strategic planning is not "spiritual"—is simply a tactic to avoid the hard work of doing the job well.

Just as we would not send a letter to people asking them to have a Holy Lent, and then hope for the best; so too, we cannot send a letter about pledging and simply sit back and hope the money rolls in. It is as much a responsibility for the church to ask and to plan the way it asks as it is for the parishioner to give. When we plan a program over the course of a year, with specific dates and specific responsibilities assigned to specific people, the job gets done *and* the people flourish.

What—and How—Are You Planning?

A successful stewardship program involves the following elements, all of which require planning:

1. Clergy committed to helping the people of their parish deal with their money in the context of their relationship with God
2. Wardens willing to support their clergy as they help with the spiritual formation of the people
3. A formation program that fosters growth around stewardship among all baptized persons year round

4. A program for the annual pledge campaign that has a specific beginning, a six- to eight-week period of discernment and case-communication with the congregation and a specific ending

5. Specific programs of education and spiritual formation, and periods of time for prayer and open conversation, about our relationship with money and with God

6. A communications plan

Five Points for Strategic Planning

Knowing those steps, here are the five keys to strategic campaign planning, the ones you absolutely cannot miss:

1. *Look back*
By looking hard at the past, we do not repeat the mistakes of the past in the present and future. The chairperson of a Stewardship Campaign Ministry should keep a binder (even if it is all on a computer) with all Stewardship Campaign materials and notes throughout the year. The same binder should include samples of all documents, communications, mailings and campaign materials such as pledge cards, brochures and bulletin inserts, along with notes about what went well, what did not go well and what you suggest be done differently next year. At the end of the campaign this binder should be appended with an evaluation of the campaign.

Even computer files should be printed in hard copy for archives. It is also valuable to consider duplicating a campaign binder so that one can be placed in the church archives and the other made available to the next year's campaign committee or chairperson.

2. *Know the numbers*
Do not be deluded into thinking that managing a church and a stewardship campaign is a spiritual task that does not require basic management tools. We both pray for the mountain to be moved *and* bring a shovel.

In this case, that means each campaign committee, vestry and clergy/staff or other church staff/leadership team should be familiar with recent numbers and should be able to discuss them easily and quickly in a vestry meeting and with a congregant.

Data all key leaders should have on hand at all times:
- Average pledge
- Number of pledging units
- Average Sunday attendance (ASA)
- Number of pledgers who need special requests (i.e., major donors)

Dates to be memorized and available:
- Campaign Kickoff Celebration
- Campaign Victory Celebration
- Annual meeting (at which a review of effectiveness is offered back to the congregation and a case for next year is delivered, based on feedback given by the congregation in planning interviews and questionnaires)

Congregants are looking for transparency, and not having basic statistics and dates available could easily be misinterpreted as obfuscation, when in fact it is simply bad planning. Campaign committees and vestries need to have the following basic information available and should be looking each year at how one set of numbers compares to the next year's goals and outcomes:
- Average pledge
- Average Sunday attendance
- Number of pledges increased/decreased
- Number of new pledges
- Number of pledges lost to death, departure or dissatisfaction
- Amount raised last year
- Number of new members
- Enrolment in primary formation opportunities
- Number of congregants involved in outreach ministries
- Number of congregants involved in in-reach ministries
- Significant situations of conflict or misconduct that might affect giving (names need not be divulged but issues must be)
- Number of new members in the planned giving legacy society
- Gift acknowledgement process (thank-you letters)

It is relatively easy to create a simple spreadsheet that captures numbers from the model evaluation and runs them side by side with columns for increase and decrease and even one for projections for the next year. This spreadsheet—which can be shared with the vestry, clergy and wider-church leadership—will clearly demonstrate the effectiveness of the campaign and its leadership. There should be no resistance to providing this level of clarity, management reporting and transparency.

The evaluation form on page 153 in Chapter 12 represents a simple, effective way to collect that information, both in numbers and in narrative.

3. *Plan ahead*

Campaign planning checklists like the models in "Part IV: The Campaign" are essential tools for creating and working your plan. If a pledge campaign has an October 15 start-date, then a strategic plan needs to be developed by February (or five non-summer and non-December months prior to the campaign kickoff). That strategic plan needs to be updated monthly, basically whenever the status is being reported to the vestry.

4. *Set public and internal goals*
There are public and internal goals to any campaign, and a stewardship campaign is no different.

The amount of money raised should *not* be a public goal, and even if it is an internal goal it should be kept open. Why? Because there is always the possibility that you could raise more money! Too often a church will set a goal based on the budget needs for the following year; this planning is laudable, but more appropriate for management projections. I suggest that the emphasis be placed not on the amount to be raised, and rather on the case (that is, the mission to be funded) and the donors (that is, the people who pledge, based on their spiritual depth and levels of church involvement).

If you announce, "We need to raise $89,000," then you will limit the congregation and the church to that amount. As you reach that goal, the campaign will slow, effectively abandoning those who could pledge more or have yet to pledge. Yes, the rector and vestry should know what amount is needed to maintain a church budget (an internal goal), and if asked they should freely note that amount.

By keeping the amount you expect to raise open, you are saying, in effect, "If the Holy Spirit really catches fire, and we do amazing work in spiritual depth, description of the mission and involvement of the people in that mission; and if, as a result, giving increases; then we welcome twice what we raised last year and will deal with that crisis by increasing mission and ministry!"

People invest in a church that deserves the money being raised. If massive shortfalls occur, it is possible that the people are voting with their money and saying either they do not know what the money is being used for *or* they do not support what the money is being used for. It is the job of the clergy and vestry to communicate effectively regarding mission and vision, accomplishments and successes throughout the year, so that by the time people are asked, they are excited to make the investment in the future of the church.

5. *Celebrate and give thanks*
Plan to be exhausted at the end of the stewardship campaign. We cannot overestimate how emotionally and even spiritually exhausting it is to deal with such emotionally charged issues as money and church.

It is important to manage a process (the months before and after the campaign) and a stewardship campaign (the actual weeks of kickoff, pledge collection and celebration) in such a way that your energy is paced. Too often the campaign ends with a dull thud as soon as the money is raised, with little creative thought as to how to thank and celebrate with the people who have worked hard to solicit and make their pledges.

It is tempting to think, "Well, we raised the money. Let's just get on with ministry." Be aware: thanking people with a huge party at the end of a campaign (as at the beginning) is part of doing ministry. It brings people together for celebration and thanksgiving, reminds them of the mission around which they have gathered.

Alternately, if a campaign is not going well, keep the party on the calendar, and follow through with one of these two options:

1. Have the party anyway and use the opportunity to better explain what the money being raised is used for and why this is so important and valuable an investment of philanthropy or
2. Use the upcoming party date to call members and ask for increased pledges or ask for non-pledgers to make their pledge.

Then manage a thank-you process worthy of the people's gifts. The Society for the Prevention of Cruelty to Animals (SPCA) will send five different thank you's for a $50 gift, because it is an opportunity to tell you what the SPCA is doing and why your gift is so vital to accomplishing those goals. Why, if the average American pledge to church is $1,600, would we not make the same effort?

It is simply impossible to thank people too much. People love to be thanked for what they do and what they give. The attitude that church donors need not be thanked for doing their moral and spiritual duty is abusive and disconnected from the norms of effective nonprofit management.

The same is true for how we send pledge updates. We do not send bills or invoices to our members; we send thank-you letters. The letter may be mail-merge and may have all the information you would find in a pledge invoice (amount paid, amount due, etc.), but enfolding that information in the context of a thank-you letter is the way to get this job done.

The Year-Long Campaign Ministry Plan

By the time you finish tending to the points above and the steps outlined in the next two chapters, you will have a complete and comprehensive Campaign Ministry Plan. This plan complements the larger church calendar and sets out, in writing, what is to be done, at what time and by whom. The smallest parishes as well as the largest parishes need a campaign plan, even if the contents vary. A plan can begin with the worksheet on page 73, which sets out the basics and then can serve as a resource for building the larger plan.

A good at-a-glance planning tool is the model checklist that follows:

Campaign Ministry Plan
Checklist

Church: _____   Year: _____

Chair: _____

Members: _____

_____

_____

_____

Compelling vision statement for new income:

_____

_____

_____

_____

Dates for six planning meetings:

_____ April   _____ August

_____ May   _____ September

_____ June   _____ November

Date for campaign review and evaluation: _____ December

Dates for six Sundays   Themes   Speakers (ministry minutes)

1 _____   _____   _____

2 _____   _____   _____

3 _____   _____   _____

4 _____   _____   _____

5 _____   _____   _____

6 _____   Consecration (final) Sunday   _____

(Note: Thanksgiving week is a good week in which to have the final Sunday.)

Case Development:

Forms: _____

Author: _____

Due:_____

Kickoff Celebration: Victory Celebration:

Date:_____ Time: _____   Date: _____ Time: _____

Theme: _____   Theme: _____

Chair for food/fun: _____   Chair for food/fun: _____

Goal for attendance: _____   Goal for attendance: _____

Communications plan/dates:

Com. #1 _____

Com # 2 _____

Com # 3 _____

RSVP list: _____

Communications plan/dates:

Com. #1 _____

Com # 2 _____

Com # 3 _____

RSVP list: _____

Goals (for pledges made in one year, to be paid in following year):

Last year

All vestry pledged? _____

fall % congregation pledged_____

pledges_____

increased _____

average pledge _____

Current year

All vestry pledged? _____

fall % of pledging _____

goal # of pledges _____

increased _____

average pledge _____

Checklist (best practices):

___ all vestry/clergy has pledged

___ liturgical changes made to mix things up

___ celebration and conversion stressed

___ consider percentage of giving to income

___ pledge cards picked up and mailed

___ time and care given to discernment

___ brief Ministry Minutes/testimonies

___ pledge cards

‗‗

## CHAPTER 8

Pre-Campaign Discernment

It is quite often the case that a parish's leadership will complain about a lack of financial support from parishioners. Leaders may be tempted to say, "Our parishioners are not investing in this parish and yet we know them to be generous givers in other places." Quite often, members are not pledging because . . .

1. the church does not have a powerful vision that inspires investment;
2. the congregation's leaders have not communicated effectively the mission and vision nor have they involved the congregation in setting those priorities;
3. the members are not involved in the day-to-day ministries of the church, and so have less of a stake; or
4. the members know the ministries but simply are not passionate about them.

People are discerning, and wealthy people are both discerning and strategic with their money. If they sense the church is not the right place to put their money for these or other reasons, they will divert funding to more effective agencies, regardless of their theology around giving back to God and even regardless of their love of their church.

Members need to see that the leadership has taken time to pray and plan for the church's future. They also need to see that due time and consideration have been given to self-study, a neighborhood listening process, demographic study and other research and discernment activities. See the Member Questionnaire, the Survey and Study of Specific Ministries, and the Community Leader Interviews forms that follow.

Research and Listening Campaign (January)

Do not be afraid to get direct input from the congregation about how things are going. Members who feel their opinions are welcome and are given a clear means by which to express those thoughts will not only provide valuable insights; they will also feel more invested and therefore more willing to follow their opinions with their pledges. Donors in any nonprofit who feel shut out of planning and vision-making will invariably hold back on their philanthropy.

It is also valuable for the vestry to visit with community leaders to get their input. They may not be able to do this annually, but some do make this listening process an annual discipline to their great advantage. It accomplishes a few things:

1. Community Leadership Interviews send a message to the congregants that the church's leadership is not managing in an ivory tower, but is instead actively seeking data that integrates the mission and ministry of the church with the needs and experiences in the larger community.
2. Among community leaders, the interviews dispel notions of exclusivity and mission competition, and also send a message that the church seeks to collaborate for good and for economies of scale.
3. The interviews also provide valuable insights regarding perceptions of your church. Some may be wrong, but the fact that they exist means you need to begin to change them.
4. The interviews collect valuable data about changing trends, new growth, shifting demographics, new and planned initiatives and events, potential grants and more.
5. A process like this is usually required for grant applications, especially those based on community impact.
6. Simply entering people's offices and homes for conversation helps the church to make friends and connect with its community.

Having done this planning, the vestry can develop a powerful vision for ministries that respond directly to the needs within and beyond the congregation. The budget, case and the campaign plan will flow from there.

RESOURCE

Member Questionnaire

These questions may be posed in a series of adult forums, with a leader posted at each table to take notes. The questionnaire may also be circulated in hard copy or via e-mail and returned to the church leadership.

Name(s): _____ Date: _____

1. Over this past year, what aspect of our church's life has excited, interested or motivated you the most?

2. In what areas of church life have you noticed the Holy Spirit particularly at work? Where do you sense energy and vitality?

3. What requires the attention of your vestry or rector? Of what should they be aware? What would you like to change?

4. What task or goal should be a priority for our church over the next three years? What is the congregation doing to serve God and the local community?

5. What keeps you coming to this church? What might attract newcomers?

6. In what ministry would you like to become more involved?

7. What could we do to improve communications in the church?

8. What could we do to improve stewardship and planned giving programs in the church?

■ ■

Survey and Study
of Specific Ministries

The vestry divides the ministries of the church that deal with community care (or "in-reach"), mission and outreach. In a small parish, where there may be fewer ministries, the vestry may break into small groups with each group taking on the study of a set of ministries.

The questions for each ministry might include the following:

1. How is this ministry changing the lives of people who benefit from it?

2. What members are engaged in this ministry, either as volunteers or as donors? How are their lives affected?

3. Who is providing the ministry, and how much is this costing from the budget?

4. What more could the church be doing in this area? What unmet needs exist and what would meeting those needs require, in human and financial terms?

5. What do recipients of this ministry say about how they are being ministered to?

6. How does this ministry affect the way non-churched people see our church? What is our reputation and image?

Community Leader Interviews

Each vestry member should interview no more than five leaders or community members. Each should have a set of questions that apply to all and a few questions that are tailored to the individual being interviewed. If the session is to be recorded, the guest should be informed and asked for permission. If notes are being taken, we suggest revising them immediately after the interview, when images and phrases are most fresh.

Interview Preparation

1. List your community leaders:

   a. School

   b. Police

   c. Political

   d. Social services

   e. Civic organizations

   f. Health

   g. Planning

   h. Other religious leaders

   i. Business (i.e., café staff, grocery store owners, gas station attendants, bank tellers, etc.)

2. Divide the list among the vestry or leadership team based on the best relationships/affinity.

3. Set deadlines for visits made and for receipt of written transcriptions or summaries of answers to questions.

4. In setting appointments:

   a. ask for a specific time and date for an interview

   b. tell them what amount of time you are asking for (generally thirty minutes)

   c. be clear that you are a leader in the community through your church and are seeking their perspective on the city or town

The Interview

Set appointments, ask questions and take notes. Some questions may include:

1. What trends and challenges do you see in our community today?

2. What demographic changes do you see?

3. What social changes do you see?

4. What unmet needs exist in our community?

5. What impressions do you have of our congregation?

6. What should we know about ourselves as a church? As a diocese? As a denomination? What do you see about us that you think we may not see?

7. What reputation do our clergy have in this area?

8. What do you notice about faith communities in this area, in general?

9. Would you consider partnering with our church for the good of the community? Why or why not?

10. What are a faith community's social and cultural responsibilities today?

11. Where do you think this church's gifts and the community's needs overlap?

How to Conduct the Interview

1. Be prepared for awkward silences, and try not to interrupt or to offer your perspective. Never argue or even challenge their views if you disagree or think there are inaccuracies. You are there only to listen and report; if there is misinformation, then your church's communications ministry needs improvement.

2. Be prepared for some push-back or anger, which may trace to personal problems or past experiences of trauma with other churches. In this event, do not attempt to solve the problems on the spot. Instead, end the conversation as soon as possible and write up a set of notes immediately for the files, with a flag if the person indicates they would not like to be visited again.

3. Tend the clock well, which means holding no more than three meetings in a day, not cramming rushed meetings into a busy day.

Following the Interview

1. Write a report within twenty-four hours of the meeting, preferably within one hour.
2. Send a thank-you note to the person who made time for the interview, in order to seal the new relationship.
3. Assemble the reports for the planning session. Keep the reports confidential. Destroy recordings if they have been made.

Discernment of Call and Communication (February–March)

Use this time to conduct more interviews or to host more public, group discernment sessions. When the listening is complete, one document can be assembled as an executive summary for the vestry and/or finance committee as they plan for the following year's budget.

The document would provide the results of the member questionnaire, the ministry self-study and the interviews with local leaders. Include what the parish is doing, how the parish is spending its money and to what extent more could be done to meet basic human needs as the hands and feet of Christ.

Note: Since February usually includes part of Lent, this is an especially good month to pray about discernment, perhaps even during the liturgy. You can invite the entire church into the process of praying for and reflecting on the vision for the future.

Be sure to find ways to communicate that the congregation's input is valuable and that their mark has been made in planning the program budget.

CHAPTER 9

■■

Planning the Annual Pledge Campaign

When managing and implementing a stewardship campaign, 70 percent of the work is in planning and communications, which should have been spread over the months prior to a fall kickoff. By the time you reach the campaign launch, only 30 percent of the work—the campaign itself—will be left. Poor planning and procrastination simply make life harder for everyone and will needlessly jeopardize a program that is essential for both the conversion of the congregants and the funding of the church's mission.

Campaign Plan and Assessment (April–May)

If a parish desires to run the six-week Stewardship Campaign from mid-October through Thanksgiving (which is the suggested timeframe), then the Stewardship Ministry Committee must begin its planning in April and May. Printed materials and the recruitment of speakers must happen well in advance of the September rush.

Activities in April regarding the Annual Pledge Campaign may include the following:

1. Recruitment and confirmation of committee membership
2. Study of previous year's statistics and campaign evaluations (see Model)
3. Definition of responsibilities
4. Dialogue with the finance committee regarding budget, mission and vision

5. Consider who, if anyone, is to be asked for major gifts
6. Draft a Stewardship Campaign timetable that covers May through December
7. Recruit speakers to offer brief testimonies as part of the Ministry Minutes program
8. Draft a campaign brochure and pledge card for printing during the summer
9. Recruit and prepare a special events subgroup to design and implement the Kickoff and Victory events

When it comes to actually raising the money, a basic step in all fundraising and stewardship campaign planning is the assessment of "capacity and interest." These terms are familiar to those managing capital campaigns, planned giving programs and major gifts programs, but they are also important for stewardship campaigns. The fact is, major gifts usually make up the top tier of gifts and need to be handled carefully, strategically and sensitively.

We should begin with definitions:

Capacity: the financial assets and income of an individual. Annual campaigns usually draw from income, whereas capital, major gifts and planned giving campaigns usually draw from assets. A person with a low income and no assets has "low capacity." A person with high income and/or high assets has "high capacity."

Interest: the level of involvement and interest the prospective donor has for the organization. A person involved in many programs of the church and who attends Sunday services regularly is a person with "high interest." A person who has been on the mailing list for years but never attends is a person of "low interest." A person outside the church is a person of "very low interest," unless a ministry of the church meets a specific social or other need beloved to the donor in question.

Generally speaking, the annual Stewardship Campaign pays little attention to *capacity*; however, *interest* is very important in determining how to approach each prospective donor. While churches are nervous about tailoring the approach, other nonprofits know each donor needs to be considered according to his or her level of interest, with the hope that both the pledge and the interest (involvement) increase over time.

Ideally, the church will have a group that considers each member and affiliated member and plans strategies to grow deeper, meaningful attendance and involvement in formation, teaching, fellowship and service. That group might move through the congregational roster, asking questions like these about each person in each household:

Involvement Assessment

1. In what church programs or activities is this person currently involved? At what level?
2. In what other civic organizations is this person involved?
3. In what is this person interested? What are his/her gifts and talents? (Note: This information may come from an annual gifts and talents survey.)
4. What is the next level of deeper involvement for this person?
5. Who is the best person to invite such deeper involvement?
6. When will this invitation and conversation take place?
7. When did we last thank this person and how?
8. When did we last ask this person's opinions about matters in the church?

In smaller churches, the vestry, leadership team, or at least a clergy person with the warden or a trusted member may meet regularly to engage in this prayerful review of congregational engagement. Larger churches with a full-time clergy person and a small staff might use part of weekly staff meetings to move name-by-name through the roster to consider each member of each household.

If this sounds like an optional process, it is not. The church not attending to strategic work in deepening involvement and listening to the desires of the people will close its doors within a decade or two, due to lack of funding and lack of volunteerism.

One way to manage this process is to design a spreadsheet like the one below or to create a binder or computer file within which each person in the congregation has a dedicated space with chronological notes regarding involvement and engagement, as well as strategy and the responsible party's next step.

Samples

Involvement Moves Management
SAMPLE Spreadsheet

Parishioner	Currently Involved in	Interests	Next-step recruitment	Responsible Party/deadline
Doe, Jane	Hospital, YMCA	Marketing, gardens	Communications Committee	Sarah Jameson, June
Jones, Dave	Little League	Teaching	Sunday School	Sr. Warden/ July
Drummond, Charles	United Way	Pottery, Cooking	Hospitality & Parish potlucks	Henry James/ Advent

Involvement Moves Management
Spreadsheet

Parishioner	Currently Involved in	Interests	Next-step recruitment	Responsible Party/deadline

The spreadsheet (p. 87) is for tracking the congregation as a whole and has only the most basic information on it. The status sheet (p. 90) has more information and can help a clergy/leadership team manage more detailed conversations to move a person deeper along the path to involvement and participation as well as the good stewardship of gifts and talents. The art of leadership is matching the right person with the right task or volunteer position. Just filling rosters will only get tasks accomplished but may erode parishioner's enjoyment and, ultimately, their long-term involvement. In our rush to get rosters filled and duties covered, we are too often looking at institutional needs rather than at human capacity and interests. Making this mistake too often will erode many aspects of involvement and congregational wellness. Having used the above model(s) for your own use in tracking the parishioner's involvement and maintaining the use of it for regular staff meetings or clergy/warden meetings to follow progress and manage expectations, the following can be set up for each congregant or the following document can be used instead of the previous moves management spreadsheet. In a large church a simple data program can be developed or existing volunteer or development software used, but in most parishes this form is simply photocopied and used in a binder to manage the deepening of involvement.

Sample—Moves Management for Involvement—status sheet

Name: Smith, Josephine

Basic Stats: born 8/29/63, married, working full time, member since 1978, married here

Current involvement: vestry member, garden committee

Interests: gardening, flowers, special events, history, reading, baking

Next step for deepening involvement: enroll in Education for Ministry program

Responsible party and date due: John Smith will invite her family to dinner and discuss EFM no later than June 15 of this year. The rector will visit in Advent.

Sample WORKSHEET

Name: _____ _____

Basic Stats: _____

_____

_____

Current involvement: _____

_____

_____

Interests: _____

_____

_____

Next step for deepening involvement: _____

_____

_____

Responsible party and date due: _____

_____

_____

■ ■

Most assessment sessions in which capacity is discussed are related to major gifts programs or campaigns, capital campaigns and planned giving programs. Clearly, the discussion of a person's financial assets and income requires the highest sensitivity, absolute confidentiality and institutional trust. This work is usually done by a committee of no more than two or three people who are both trusted by the congregation. Their conversations take about three minutes per person and are not recorded, and their notes are strictly confidential.

The combination of capacity and interest determines a pledge of any level to anything, regardless of whether that is a pledge of money, time or support. Here is how it works.

A person of:

High capacity and low interest = a person who is wealthy and uninvolved or uninterested

Low capacity and low interest = a person who is not wealthy and uninvolved or uninterested

High capacity and high interest = a person who is wealthy and very connected to your church with high involvement and high awareness about mission

Low capacity and high interest = a person who is not wealthy but is very connected to your church with high involvement and high awareness about mission

Please note that the term "wealthy" is relative. In a small, rural church the term may simply mean a family or person with means beyond subsistence, some of whose resources may be able to be given away. Churches often fall into the delusion that there are no people or few people with wealth in their congregation. This projection of anxiety debilitates stewardship and denies donors the ability to make larger gifts to the church. In many churches, especially in New England and the Midwest, wealthy people work hard not to appear wealthy. This is even more the case among Generations X and Y for whom certain symbols of wealth hold little importance.

This is no sinister invasion of privacy, nor is it an attempt to sort sheep from goats, or to only cultivate "high capacity" givers. Different strategies are appropriate for different situations. This is simply one of many necessary management tools in the tool box of an effective nonprofit leader.

Campaign Communications Planning (April–August)

Communication is as important to stewardship programs as rain is important to a garden. Often the greatest disconnect between a congregation and a stewardship program, capital campaign, major gifts initiative or planned giving effort involves poor communication.

In a small church of fewer than twenty members, communications may be as simple as a leaflet and a series of presentations and bulletin inserts. For a larger church, an entire plan with multiple avenues should be designed and executed by a staff that includes some expertise in communications.

The important thing is that there be a plan—regardless of whether it is expensive and massive or inexpensive and lean. And it is essential that the plan be executed on schedule in order to communicate the mission and an invitation to give.

If it is possible, one person on the Stewardship Ministry Committee should be responsible for communications. Ideally that person should have some background in the area of strategic communications, either professionally or as a volunteer; at the least, they should have a passion for connecting people.

Even with great volunteer support, you will still need a budget for the Stewardship Campaign and planning program. It can be large or small, depending on each church's program design and resources, which is why no model budget is proposed herein.

There will be those who object to or are even outraged by the use of a printed or photocopied brochure, insisting it is too slick and professional for use in a parish. The reality is that these days, a one-page sheet folded twice can be crafted on an average personal computer by a person with average design skills in less than an hour and can be copied on colored paper for a modest amount.

What is also true is that, whether we like it or not, the church is not the only institution to which people are being asked to give money. The church can neither afford to stick its head in the sand and pretend that these other organizations are "wrong" or "too commercial," nor can the church say it is too spiritual to have to communicate well.

The following list captures most of the communications tools that are valuable to design and produce over the course of the spring and summer for a fall campaign:

RESOURCE

Advanced Communications Toolkit

1. Standard campaign brochure

2. Signed statement of tithing by clergy and vestry

3. Stories of new and innovative mission and outreach initiatives

4. Photos and statements from "Ministry Minutes" speakers

5. A letter from the vestry outlining the campaign

6. One or more photographs

7. Newsletter articles

8. Blog entries

9. A collect or meditation to help people praying about their pledge

10. A series of announcements about the final campaign event

11. A reference to the enclosed pledge card

12. Website references for pledging online

13. The pledge card (8½" by 11" heavy stock paper, 12–14 point font)

14. Bulletin inserts

15. Posters and flyers

16. Sermon titles or sermon series

17. Reminder notices

18. Campaign status announcements

19. Letters, cards and postcards for gift acknowledgement and event promotion

20. Invitations, save-the-date cards and other announcements and reminders

21. Campaign reports

Not one of these communications tools should be designed during the campaign. With a campaign of two months, there are ten months left in which to design and ready each of these tools as long as campaign managers pace themselves and take on one design initiative at a time many months before the campaign begins. Winter, spring and summer are months for design, production and implementation.

Even in a small parish with twenty-five congregants and a priest working quarter-time, a talented communicator with an average computer can generate attractive, user-friendly communications tools in the ten months leading up to the campaign. One person working two hours per week for thirty weeks can single-handedly lead an effective annual stewardship campaign in a small church with limited resources and still employ most of the key traits to effective fundraising in this book.

If you have to work smart (not hard) because of limited resources, then focus on these tools first and then do others as time and resources permit:

Essential Communications Toolkit

1. Attractive, large-print, large paper format pledge card

2. Eight bulletin inserts (same format, different content)

3. The campaign Kickoff Celebration invitation series (to also include Victory Celebration date)

   a. Save the date card (six months in advance)

   b. Reminder card (three months in advance)

   c. Invitation (one month in advance)

   d. Letter to encourage attendance to non-registrants (two weeks in advance)

   e. Reminder card (one week in advance)

4. Poster-size image showing percentage of Average Sunday Attendance pledging and progress to 100 percent pledging

5. Web page for posting all print materials

6. The campaign Victory Celebration event invitation series

   a. Save the date card (sent with Kickoff announcement)

   b. Reminder save the date card (sent with Kickoff announcement)

   c. Invitation (one month in advance)

   d. Letter to encourage attendance to non-registrants (two weeks in advance)

   e. Reminder card (one week in advance)

7. Thank-you letter and copy for rector's hand-written notes

8. Campaign conclusion article for the newsletter and website

9. Template for billing (in thank-you letter format)

10. Year-end tax thank-you letters

Spread over ten months this work will require approximately two hours per month, and even less time if diocesan human resources (for instance, a canon for Stewardship and Financial Development) are applied to assisting small parishes.

Special Events

What stuns me most of all about how the church does fundraising and discusses stewardship is that it is entirely too funereal. We work with the bleak attitude of a Victorian workhouse board, like the one in Charles Dickens's *Oliver Twist*. We are so frightened of fundraising that our speed to get past it robs us of having some fun along the way.

Many of our churches are very small, so the best plan is to recruit one or two people who are well known for hospitality and one younger person who is gifted in creative thinking and/or technology. Then give them the *sole* task of handling the special events of the campaign.

Not only do special events bring joy into the process, they also bring people together, strengthen community and provide a forum for educating members about mission, budget and church life in ways that a dull annual meeting could never accomplish.

Events that put the "Fun" in Fundraising

1. The year in review—a slide show of the past year in the church's life

2. A local celebrity as speaker or host

3. A food-related theme, especially if a parishioner has a restaurant or a particular expertise—Indian, Thai, Chinese Dim Sum, Southwestern, barbecue, soul food, etc.

4. Potluck diners are fun and easy, but why not add a twist with a theme?

    a. Chocolate potlucks

    b. Appetizer potlucks

    c. Homemade breads with interesting spreads

    d. Chili cook-off

    e. French bistro

    f. English tea

    g. Soups and breads

    h. Salads and breads

    i. All things Middle Eastern—think of the Last Supper

    j. A martyr's dinner (red things)

    k. A shepherd's potluck—things made with lamb

    l. A family potluck—only family recipes

5. A meal of roasted meat (cooked by everyone's favorite cook in the congregation) with potluck sides brought by alphabetical groupings (everyone with a last name of A through D, bring breads; E through K, bring salads; etc.)

6. Pit barbecue is easier than it sounds. You can create a pit with cinder-block, steel bars and wire grates, to easily cook pit-roasted meats and vegetables for many people at once. A barbeque pit will cost

$150 to make and is a great way to bring a community together for large meals.

7. Pizza night is easy if you set up the dough in advance, par-bake the pizza crusts with a basic red sauce, have cheese set aside, and then let people bring toppings as the potluck and run pizzas into the oven through the evening.

8. Baked potato bar with stations for fixings

9. Omelet brunch bar

10. Apple-themed dinner with a recipe book as the invitation

11. Mardi Gras complete with costumes, a parade and Creole foods

12. Dinner and dancing from a certain era (The Roaring Twenties, Fifties Sock-hop, Disco Night)

13. Ice cream social

14. Marching bands

15. Christmas in September

16. Episodes of favorite television shows or movie clips about giving

17. Skits by youth about giving

18. "Church Lady" skits (remember Dana Carvey's character on Saturday Night Live?)—this time she is complaining about all this talk about stewardship (humor is a great way to face into resistance)

19. Olympic giving (use the music and medals for generosity, etc.)

20. Thanksgiving themes

21. A coffee hour treat, like made-to-order omelets, crepe stations or trifle stations

Once you are ready to dive into the planning, this questionnaire will help to guarantee that you are on the right track in your event planning:

Special Event Planning Questionnaire

1. What do you hope to gain through this event? Each event needs to have three primary elements to its planning:

   a. What is so fun about it that exhausted people will give up a night on the couch?

   b. What is the one thing you want people to go home having learned or been inspired toward?

   c. What is the one action you are going to ask them to take?

2. Does this event have a hook—something that is intriguing or interesting or new?

3. What is the budget for this event and is that budget in keeping with the church and the tone of the event? Is it fun without being extravagant?

4. Does the event teach something about the church, community, campaign, mission or ministry?

5. Do you have the people available to get the job done?

6. Do you have a marketing plan for the event that will provide a series of creative and attractive invitations (save-the-date cards, invitation, reminder, letter of invitation, teaser, last-minute reminder)?

7. Does the event have a moment of decision in it, and what is it that you want attendees to decide?

8. Will the event offer an external public awareness or is this purely an internal event?

9. Are there any competing events in town or within the church?

10. Do you have an executive summary of the event that takes the leaders through every minute of the evening from one hour before the start to one hour after the end of the event?

And as the event gets closer, be sure you have all of your checklists in place:

1. Invitations

2. Scheduling

3. Creative menus and decorations

4. Publicity

5. Set-up

6. Clean-up

7. Gifts to those attending

8. Entertainment

9. Worship or prayers

10. Program or content

11. Messaging or goal for a decision made by attendees

When it comes to event planning, 70 percent of the effort goes into getting people to attend; the remaining 30 percent will be sufficient to create an enjoyable and meaningful time. Lots of fine work to throw a grand party will be meaningless if people do not attend. So make an ambitious communications plan and put plenty of energy into it in order to get onto your members' radar. Over time, a well-planned and joy-filled event will gain its own reputation and become institutionalized within the church as a "don't miss" event.

Campaign Checklist

When your plans are in place—not yet fully executed, but in place—you will be ready to assemble a complete Campaign Checklist. You might use the model that follows.

RESOURCE

Stewardship Campaign Checklist

Date	Action	Responsible Person	Location	Notes
	Recruit Ministry Team			
	Work out dates for campaign and meetings			
	• set and communicate			
	• reserve rooms			
	Assemble materials templates			
	Sketch Kickoff event			
	Sketch Victory event			
	Design campaign visuals			
	Create involvement thermometer			
	Create pledge card			
	• design card			
	• produce card			
	• compose pledge card letter			
	Organize Ministry Minutes			
	• recruit participants			
	• photos for brochure			

Date	Action	Responsible Person	Location	Notes
	• statements for brochure			
	• print brochure			
	Coordinate vestry pledge			
	• pledge statement			
	• pledge presentation			
	Arrange liturgical presence			
	• sermon placement			
	• liturgical coordination			
	Hold Kickoff Celebration			
	• space			
	• food			
	• invitations/marketing			
	• speaker			
	• checklist			
	Send weekly mailings			
	Phone non-pledgers			
	Hold Victory Event			
	• space			
	• food			
	• invitations/marketing			
	• speaker			
	• checklist			
	Organize gratitude effort			
	• compose and send thank-you notes			
	• compose and send thank-you letters			

Date	Action	Responsible Person	Location	Notes
	Recognize volunteers			
	Evaluate campaign			
	Issue final report to congregation			
	Organize for next campaign			
	• next campaign chair			
	• next campaign calendar			

■ ■

PART IV

The Campaign

CHAPTER 10

■ ■

The Case for Support

What you have read so far has hopefully raised your awareness that the primary work of fundraising is letting go of the fear: fear of giving, fear of asking, fear of the campaign itself. If you plan well, the actual Pledge Campaign is relatively simple and straightforward and nothing to fear.

Church fundraising is like aviation, in that it needs:

- Careful attention to the assembling of the parts (committee formation and planning)
- Careful mathematical work on the flight plan (the campaign plan, case-for-support and to-do lists)
- A clear-headed and determined pilot (the fearless, centered, well-prayed chair)
- A very long runway (the spring-to-summer creation and set-up of tools, such as pledge cards, flyers, invitations, bulletin inserts, etc.)

Once you have these things, the flight is actually short and uneventful. Try to cut corners on any of the set-up and the entire flight may be jeopardized.

The campaign itself, whether in a massive church with lots of resources or a small church of twenty dedicated souls—is rather basic. There are options around themes, artwork, event planning and design, but the nuts and bolts are common. So take a deep breath as we move through the actual campaign step by step.

Craft the Case

In fundraising terms, the answer to the query, "Why we are raising this money?" is called the "case for support." This case is the description (in print, video, sermon, presentation at a church meeting, etc.) of what the church is doing to change the world. In small churches, in which the clergy compensation and building expenses form the bulk of the budget, the case for support simply needs to translate that set of numbers into ministry that the donor can vividly imagine.

The case for support needs to so move the donor that he or she decides to fund this vision rather than funding the compelling cases presented by other organizations. Those groups have been busy saving lives and feeding millions. What have you been up to?

The case for support need not be long or complex. In fact it is best if it is neither; all you need is five hundred words and related, high-quality imagery. The case simply states, in a few paragraphs, what the money is helping to accomplish and why the donor should give (make an investment) in this church.

Please do not over-spiritualize your church or its mission. At the end of the day, people have a finite amount of money to pledge to those entities they love and appreciate. Your church is one of many nonprofits, so you must match your conversion-oriented preaching with the managerial skill to help donors choose your ministry—not because it is holy but because it is worthy of funding.

Ideally, the budget of a parish is set through prayer and other hard work based on a vision of what needs to be accomplished in the life of the parish. The Holy Spirit has a hope for your parish. The work of the clergy and vestry is to discern what the hope of the Holy Spirit is and to make a budget that reflects that hope. The budget should not be limited to "what we absolutely have to get done," but should rather be reflective of the great optimism we pray for when we say "thy Kingdom come, thy will be done, on earth as it is in heaven."

The best, most successful strategy is (1) to establish what wonderful things need to be done by your parish based on active discernment and a collection of the congregation's input, (2) to communicate that vision to the people of the parish (long before you ask them for their pledges) and then (3) to ask them to fund the vision.

If you have done the "listening campaign" suggested for January and February, then you will have all you need to craft a vision that resonates with the deepest yearnings of your congregation and neighborhood partners. They will give to a vision they, themselves have been able to offer. Involvement in drafting the vision and mission is essential. In addition to those tools, you might use a letter like the one that follows to inform or remind your congregation about the good work you have been doing with their last pledge. This letter also helps to pave the way for the next pledge by getting people's input *prior* to asking for the next pledge.

Case Development—Three steps to assembling a vision *from* the people so that their discernment is welcomed, collected, reported back and used in planning. The result is donors investing in their own vision and not one imposed upon them:

1. **Host a conversation**: Every year, a process needs to be designed and implemented in which the congregation is given the opportunity to express their deepest desires for being a church. Often, churches do the same thing every few years for long-term goal and vision-setting. Too often this does not happen. Either congregations blindly follow a clergy-person or the loudest or richest or most manipulative lay leader, or all four, or some combination. *People will only give to what they themselves have been a part of building* and this is exponentially true for younger generations. The ideal mission of a parish is not inherited with new year-dates at the top of the page, but generated through the prayers, inspiration, hopes and dreams, discernment and real expressions of the people in the church. There are lots of ways to host a conversation and there is no need to feel that every idea expressed in this process must be incorporated into the vision of the church. The clergy and vestry or church leadership is charged with this fine-tuning. But every single pledger or donor needs to feel that *their opinion was asked for and was heard*. If that is truly the case, then when they are asked for money, they will sense that they are investing in something they themselves have been part of birthing. In a small church this may be as simple as the following:

   a. Dialogue sermon between a preacher and a congregation with a note-taker.

   b. A pot luck dinner-discussion about homes and dreams for the mission and ministry of the congregation's life and work together in the next year or years.

   c. A series of house-parties in which small dinner groups meet in parishioners' homes and the results are all compiled into a larger document and shared as discernment is done by the vestry.

   d. A questionnaire, in which ideas are collected, assembled and reported back.

e. A series of hosted events in which the congregation is invited to meet with the vestry in small groups for a discussion of their hopes and dreams of mission and ministry.

f. Web conferencing in which a series of webinars are hosted (though this may only be efficient among younger congregants.)

In a larger church there may be the need for a parish conference or a combination of initiatives such as:

g. A questionnaire mailer, followed by an assembled feedback-results-mailing and then a conference or parish retreat day in which the results of the questionnaire are discussed and prioritized.

h. A parish-town-hall meeting in an abbreviated liturgy so that the liturgy of the Word was this conversation about the hopes and dreams of mission and ministry followed by a brief communion.

i. Small-group speed-dating tables with large posters in the center of the table in which vestry members host at each table around a topic of conversation and the congregants are invited to move to a different table in each of a series of time periods offering input and processing previous group's ideas.

2. **Return the Input:** This part of the process of collecting discernment from the congregation is essential and is often the piece which falls through the cracks in the speed to get to the final outcomes and move on with the ministry development. If you ask congregants what they think the church should be and do, but do not tell them what you have gleaned from the conversation, they are demoralized and feel disempowered—possibly feeling manipulated into the work of telling their story without any confidence that they were listened to. Regardless if you collect ideas on index cards or collect ideas in dinner groups or collect ideas at a pot luck or at a conference such as the technology available in The Art of Hosting (http://www.artofhosting.org/home/,) it is essential that the people involved in the conversation sense that what they have contributed has been heard and returned back to them in a form which proves that the exercise was not empty or fruitless. This return of input may look like posting idea cards at the back of the church hall or listing the ideas on posters or creating an ideas list as an insert or a mailing or part of a newsletter or on a website. Regardless, collecting ideas from parishioners is only as good as showing them that you listened. You do not need to use every idea. You do need to listen to every idea.

3. **Discern the congregational input into a vision and then create and communicate a case for support**: I see "danger" flags when clergy or lay leadership do not welcome the input of the congregation or when they welcome it in manipulative ways which guide outcomes. And the congregation sees them too. And the leaders never think their congregations can see it. Congregations are very, very wise. They see what they need to see even if they find it hard to know what to do with what they see.

After the conversation is hosted, and the results are returned to the congregation, then the leadership works with the vision—that is, whatever was returned to the congregation (see number 2)—distilling and discerning the raw-data into a crafted vision and mission which they will then further craft into statements, videos, brochures, stewardship letters—ie: the case for support—communications which answer the question on which fundraising hangs: "Why should I invest in their project with my philanthropy?" There was a time, even recently, in which people would just give to the church because that was what one does in our society. But times have changed, and today we need to take these three steps when defining a case: host conversation, return data and develop/discern data into an answer to the question: "Why should I give to this church?" If the asker of this question (the donor) sees their own hand in the answer, or knows it was listened to in getting the answer, they will pledge and pledge boldly.

Case Development Survey Letter

(Church name)

(Church address)

Date

Dear Members,

As we enter the season of Lent, a natural time of discernment, your vestry is prayerfully considering the budget for next year in advance of our stewardship program next fall. We are planning a year in advance so that we are sure that the money entrusted to this parish through pledges is used in the best way possible, as we both reach in to care for people attending the parish and reach out to those in our area with whom Christ would have us minister.

As the vestry does this self-study and discernment, we would very much benefit from your input. Below we have listed in-reach and outreach ministries in our congregation, along with some basic statistical information about each ministry. After reading the list, please prayerfully consider each one and also imagine other ministries, either to our own parishioners or to people beyond our walls, that you feel we should consider.

We hope that you are interested in learning more about our shared ministries, and we're sure that your suggestions for other ministries will help us to consider the best possible use of time and money in next year's budget.

(Examples)

Food Pantry: We currently provide three bags of groceries to three families per week from September through June.

Parish Nursing: Sarah Jones visits two home-bound parishioners each week and is available to parishioners who have no health insurance.

Clergy Visitation: Clergy visit those in hospital every day and those who are home-bound every month with communion and conversation.

Child Care: Infants and toddlers attending this parish are cared for during services and major community events. This ministry involves 150 volunteer hours and fifty paid hours per year to a congregation increasingly growing with young families.

What other outreach opportunities do you see that need to be addressed, especially given the particular gifts, vision and resources of our congregation? Please feel free to communicate these to the vestry secretary (*or chair of the Stewardship Ministry*) at (*address and telephone*).

Sincerely yours,

Vestry signatures

■·■■■·■■

Please be clear about one thing: the success of the annual pledge campaign of a church is based on the firm foundation of a mission worthy of being funded. In the past, the World War II generation, the Silent Generation and the older two-thirds of the baby boomers were willing to follow the last dozen generations by giving to their church based on social and geographic affiliation. But Generations X and Y will change all that forever.

Beginning in 2015, when baby boomers begin to hand over giving and pledging to Generation X, pledges to the church will need to be deserved, for the first time in 1,700 years (in other words, since the church received the endorsement of the emperor Constantine). Even with members who may have been giving the same pledge for decades, each new year is a new opportunity to explain what your church is accomplishing and why it deserves the investment of this stewardship gift. So whether you are asking the Silent Generation or Generation Y, your case matters now in a way that it never has before.

Here are some things to tell the church members as you design your case:

Components of the Case

1. What is your purpose and mission in this place at this time?

2. Why is what you do and who you are important and to whom? What would be missed if your church ceased to exist?

3. What specific strategies does your church have to address or solve a problem or meet a need?

   a. The sick

   b. The poor

   c. The marginalized

   d. Hospitality

   e. Worship

   f. Beauty

   g. Human connection

   h. Education and formation

   i. Restoration and hope

4. What are your long- and short-term goals as a nonprofit?

5. What have been your church's accomplishments and successes?

6. What future impact does your church plan to have on an issue, group or cause?

And here are some suggestions as you develop the words and images that will make up your actual case:

RESOURCE

Composing Your Case

1. Involve a group of staff, lay leaders, congregants, youth and people unaffiliated with the church. In a very small church, consider using the whole congregation one Sunday.
2. Use only one writer (a good one with proven skills as a writer) and keep it short.
3. Use no jargon.
4. Be convincing and optimistic. (People will not give to a sinking ship nor will they give just because you need the money to build a budget or pay a clergy person.)
5. Use, as your focal point, the strengths of the church and not the needs of the budget.
6. Focus on the future and spend little time on the past.
7. Use images whenever possible and tell stories of people's lives changed whenever possible.
8. Tell a story from beginning to end.
9. Edit your case from the point of view of the donor, not the vestry or the clergy.
10. Show that the church can and will solve problems.
11. Show that making a pledge is a good investment and explain why.
12. Be able to boil the entire case down into a three-minute elevator speech of about three hundred words: a brief description of why making a pledge to your church is more than just a response to God's bounty, but also a good investment.
13. Step into the humility of asking for support.
14. Have the document or DVD draft reviewed by several eyes to ensure accuracy.

Communicating the Case

The most popular form of a case for support is the standard "priest's stewardship letter," a model of which follows, but we recommend that a case be developed that also includes testimonials and photographs. The rector's letter should never be the only nor should it be the primary vehicle for a church's case for support.

These days, it is increasingly important to craft the communications tool that will carry the case to its intended hearer. If you are reaching out to people in their thirties, then you may need to use Facebook or e-mail or a blog or web link. If you are reaching out to a person in their late seventies, a brochure with 14-point typeface and a hand-written note might be the best way to communicate.

Even in a small church of twenty people, it may be that letters are sent to the fourteen people sixty and older, while a simple website with a blog-based case is developed for the youngest six members. And it might just prove interesting to the other fourteen.

A case for support is *any* form of written or video-based explanation as to why you are raising the money. Your case for support can take any of the following forms:

What Form Will Your Case Take?

- A double-sided letter-sized sheet of paper, folded into a brochure
- A letter
- A blog or website
- A short DVD
- A few paragraphs in a bulletin describing what the church accomplishes in the world and among its members
- A skit or play describing various ways the church's ministries change lives
- A speech by a warden or a team of vestry members highlighting visible plans that rise out of next year's budget
- A series of Ministry Minutes (or testimonials) in which members describe what they love about their church
- A brochure of multiple pages with photos and copy that outlines what the church did with last year's income and how it touched lives, plus a request for next year's pledge
- A slide show or presentation describing what lives have been impacted by the church's work and ministry and requesting a pledge for the coming year
- A booklet with a series of photos showing life in the church, with a final page highlighting what next year's budget will make possible and why it should be funded

A parishioner with a camera that takes video and the most basic movie software, which comes on most computers these days, can be used to make a no-frills but perfectly adequate and often very moving video in one Sunday morning of filming and six hours of volunteer time one afternoon. Campaign videos are not just for rich churches with a camera crew anymore.

RESOURCE

Campaign Case Presentation Letter

(Inside address)

Date

Dear *(first name)*,

Every day, people living in and around *(church name)* are experiencing sustenance, growth, transformation and care through our ministries. Our rector *(name)* and wardens *(names)* have nurtured and grown our congregation alongside many lay leaders. Now, in this time of clergy transition, it is our job to move forward in strength.

It is our great privilege to serve you as the vestry and to invite you into our stewardship program this fall. We are each looking hard at our pledge to consider an increase this year, because we benefit from all that God has given to us and are grateful to return some portion to God for use in our parish life. Part of our strength is having a sound budget that shows we are excited about our mission and willing to invest in it.

The reality is also that giving is something clergy candidates consider as they evaluate our health, both spiritual and fiscal, and imagine accepting a call to join us. Our pledge is also an investment in human lives being changed. Here are just a few examples of what these funds help us to accomplish in people's lives:

- Our ministry as a community center, open to groups such as *(examples)*
- Contributions to *(examples)*
- Support of various human service initiatives *(examples)*

Our theme for this year's Stewardship Campaign is "Sustenance," as we focus on finding and funding a new priest. Your pledge provides a pastor for our sustenance:

- A person who will (*briefly describe one vivid, meaningful facet of priest's job*)
- A person who will (*briefly describe one vivid, meaningful facet of priest's job*)
- A person who will (*briefly describe one vivid, meaningful facet of priest's job*)

How can we support the sustenance and growth of these ministries and welcome truly great leadership into our midst? We ask you to pray, plan and think about your sustaining pledge for 2012, understanding that if your financial circumstances change, you can change your pledge.

We are a strong parish. We are being formed and changed into God's hope for us. Please join us in making a bold pledge this year.

Warmly and gratefully yours,

(*Signed by all committee members, no photocopied signatures*)

▪▪▪

Stewardship and fundraising shine best in the church where the world's deepest needs and the congregation's greatest joy meet. The case encourages both these events to occur.

CHAPTER 11

■■

Campaign Materials

Fear shuts creativity down, locks it up and throws away the key. Fearless fundraising allows for the kind of creativity that, though not expensive, does take time and initiative to accomplish. This is why the creative work of a campaign needs to be designed and accomplished in the spring—many months before the actual campaign. Resistance pushes the planning too late in the year to be creative. The result is that—when it becomes clear the campaign can no longer be put off—the work begins in a nervous frenzy without the time to imagine or accomplish innovative plans.

Most of the materials to be used in a campaign can be done carefully, easily and creatively as long as they are not left to the last minute. What follows is a description of exactly how the campaign unfolds and a description of the materials being used along the way. A small church of under sixty congregants, with two or three stewardship pledge campaign leaders working a well-planned campaign can easily accomplish these tasks over the course of the two months of the campaign *if* the previous ten months were employed with campaign planning, volunteer recruitment and material generation.

The Lead-up to Kickoff

Two to four weeks prior to the kickoff of the stewardship campaign, the congregation is invited to make the issue of raising money a matter of personal and corporate prayer. Prayers are inserted into the bulletins, and these prayers can be re-used year after year, especially if they are provided on glossy postcards or bookmarks.

If professional printing sounds beyond you, it is not. Thanks to online printing houses, anyone can, for a few cents per card, have an image of the church or an icon printed in full color on one side of a post card and a campaign prayer on the other. Versions without the prayer can be used for thank-you notes.

These same online printers will often also print images on puzzles and other giveaways, a fun way to remind congregants that their pledge is a part of a whole. If you go with the puzzle, you can stick a puzzle piece to each pledge card and have them place their puzzle piece onto an empty frame as part of a social or liturgical event. (Note: buy a second puzzle in case people lose their puzzle pieces... and they will.) Plan ahead—it usually takes a few weeks for delivery of these customized items.

Beginning the weeks before the campaign Kickoff, clergy and laity should discuss how the liturgies on Sundays and other celebrations will align with the fall stewardship season. Will there be collects, prayers of the people, Ministry Minutes, sermons, special announcements, special food and drink, special hymns or other music? The worst thing planners can do is to allow the liturgies to be unchanged during the campaign. Liturgies and language need to change to jolt congregants out of the norm and excite them about the journey the congregation is on together.

The Pledge Card or "Certificate"

On the first Sunday of the six- to eight-week campaign, the pledge cards are distributed. This is true regardless of whether the church is twenty or two thousand congregants.

The pledge card is the mother of all materials in a pledge campaign. I actually call the sample on the next page a pledge certificate, and I suggest you do, as well. The word "certificate" lends gravitas to the page, reminding people that it represents a holy and sacramental act, an agreement with God and the congregation.

It is worth the effort to spend time making this document attractive. Choose good and heavy paper and a beautiful image for the upper corner of the certificate. There is no need to limit yourself to your logo or the church crest. Choose a symbol like a tea bowl or a sprouting flower or an icon—some image that is in concert with your theme.

And remember: many members may need a larger typeface, so keep the type large, no smaller than twelve- to fourteen-point if possible, even if you need to go to a two-sided printing. Also be sure that the areas for writing are large enough to write legibly with ease. Tiny pledge cards are hard to manage and do not send a message of bounty in keeping with the size of the gift for which you are asking.

Information about planned giving should also be on all pledge cards, since the best time to ask for a planned gift is when people are already thinking about money. As pledge cards come in, highlight any planned giving notification and get a copy to clergy and wardens immediately for follow-up. Requests for contact about planned giving or bequests should be followed up within twenty-four hours. Clergy who lose a planned gift to a school or other nonprofit have lost an average gift of $50,000.

Sample Pledge Certificate

(*Church Name*)
(City)

Stewardship Campaign Pledge Certificate
for (following year) Offering Back to God

Name:_____

Address: _____

Home telephone: _____ Work telephone: _____

E-mail address: _____

In gratitude for all that God has given to me/us and in the awareness of all that God is calling (church name) to do in (city), in surrounding communities, the Diocese and the world, I/we would like to return a portion to God through (church name).

I/we understand that this gift is a symbol of our gratitude for life, love, health, food, shelter, talents—indeed for all that we have and enjoy.

I/we hereby pledge a total gift of

$ _____

**during the next fiscal year
(January 1, (*year*)—December 31,
(*year*).**

Payment Options (please check only one)

☐ a weekly pledge of $ _____, totaling $_____ for the year

☐ a monthly pledge of $_____, totaling $_____ for
the year

☐ a one-time gift pledge of $_____ for the year to be paid in the month
of _____

In the event of a financial problem this or next year, your pledge can be adjusted by contacting the Rector or Treasurer. You will be sent a confirmation letter, envelopes and a December letter for tax purposes.

Please send your completed pledge card to:
Stewardship Campaign, (Church), (Church Address)
or place it in an offering plate by **September 15, (year).**

Optional request of further information:

☐ I/we are interested in making a separate gift (in addition to the annual support listed above) to _____.
Please have the clergy contact me/us.

☐ I/we have made provisions in our estate plan for a planned gift to (church name).

☐ I/we are interested in receiving information about planned giving (estate planning, charitable trusts, making a will or living will, etc.). Please contact me/us and send literature to inform my/our planning.

☐ I/we are interested in making a separate gift (in addition to the annual support listed above) to (insert a specific project for which funds are needed). Please have the clergy contact us.

This Certificate is Private and Confidential.

Stewardship Campaign Kickoff Sunday

The biggest barrier to effective stewardship campaigns is boredom on the part of the congregation and laziness or resistance on the part of the leadership. Instead, when it is time to give out pledge cards during or after worship, make it a special and joyful day. I like to keep this equation in mind:

Food + fun = attention + involvement

For a host of ideas I have used or seen done to great effect, see the section on "Special Events" in Chapter 9.

The Stewardship Ministry leaders should encourage people to focus on one thing at a time. Though the calendar is packed at the start of the year, you should avoid combining the Stewardship Campaign (money) with other major events, especially the Recruitment Fair (time and talent).

At some point during this fun, first Sunday, there is work to be done:

1. Parishioners pick up their pledge cards and brochures (provided in alphabetical order in envelopes by the church door) on their way out of worship. Energy may be high, but members are asked *not* to make pledges until they have prayed for at least two weeks.

    Colored pledge cards could be included in envelopes for children to use and as a teaching tool for parents, plus a handout guiding parents in the conversation about giving. Remaining pledge cards not picked up at the Sunday Campaign Kickoff should be mailed the very next business day from the church with a "Sorry we missed you" cover letter.
2. The Sunday School and Adult Forum Hour(s) should be used for conversations and education about money. See the resources in Chapter 6 for family discussions, adult forum curricula and Sunday School plans.

Ministry Minutes

Weekly "Ministry Minutes" are a central aspect of this campaign design and cannot be underestimated for their power and impact. Churches may choose to share these testimonies using bulletin inserts or weekly mailers, in addition to in-person presentations. Here is how they work:

"Ministry Minutes" are presented as part of worship during the campaign. They are personal testimonies of how the parish has helped people in their life and Christian walk. Ministry Minutes are three to five minutes and are written and presented by parishioners, with help from clergy. The addition of Ministry Minutes demands that sermons be shortened by five minutes.

Consider these suggestions for organizing your Ministry Minutes and presenters:

- Clergy and lay leaders such as wardens or campaign leaders should identify the prospective "Ministry Minute" speakers by early August for a fall campaign. Note: it is good for clergy to be involved because they may know sensitive situations that would make it difficult for a person to speak publicly about pledging with integrity.
- Phone calls are made to ask prospective Ministry Minute speakers if they would be willing to speak on a pre-determined subject and if they are free on a scheduled Sunday to speak at all services, using a prepared and vetted speech of no more than five hundred words.
- Try to present a diversity of messages and experiences. One topic per speaker is best, such as but not limited to the following:
  — Community life
  — Beauty (liturgy, music, etc.)
  — Pastoral care
  — Worship
  — Youth ministry
  — Care for the elderly
  — Care for the sick
  — Outreach to the financially poor
  — Outreach and in-reach to the relationally and emotionally poor
- Once all six speakers are confirmed, collect photos and one-sentence message summaries from the speakers for use in the Stewardship Pledge Card Brochure or as stills in a campaign PowerPoint presentation or image-based video. If a video sounds harrowing, it need not. By using photos, you can use very basic, pre-installed programs available on most computers to make a perfectly fine and moving video. I suggest keeping the video to less than eight minutes.
- Keep talks to three minutes—that is, about 250 words or half a page single-spaced in 12-point type with one-inch margins. The script should be typed and agreed to by the speaker and coach (rector, warden, campaign chair, etc.).
- A notes version can go on a card with key speech points, so that speakers do not ramble, get paralyzed with stage-fright or obscure the message. Speakers must agree to limit the presentation to those points and the time allotted; a long Ministry Minute can be deadly to the energy of the congregation and the campaign.
- Once the speech is worked out, the coach might use the notes from the card (and a photo) for the campaign update mailing that goes out the following Monday.
- Each Sunday of the campaign, assign a different member of the Stewardship Committee to call the Ministry Minute speaker the night

before to confirm attendance, calm them down and provide last-minute coaching. The same person should also meet the speaker before worship, inform the clergy that they have arrived, and go over the service bulletin and schedule to be sure the speaker knows when to rise, speak and sit, where to stand, and how to use the microphones. In a small church it may be that one lay leader serves as point person each week for the Ministry Minute speakers.

When worship is over, the Ministry Minutes are not necessarily finished. You can also send out Ministry Minute mailings. These are simple, one-page tri-folded and sealed flyers, mailed bulk rate (if possible) the day following each featured Sunday.

These are only effective if they go out on Monday morning, so the turn-around time is fast. The Stewardship Committee should schedule to stay after church each Sunday for an hour to count and produce the statistical information which, along with the photo and quote (already collected and drafted ahead of time), helps the congregation to see the building momentum and the work of the Holy Spirit.

Ministry Minute Flyer
From This Sunday's Ministry Minute

© Djem82, Dreamstime.com

"When I was in the hospital, St. Luke's was a real source of spiritual support for me and my family. Immediately after the surgery, Rev. Keith Wilson came to the hospital and was the first face I saw when I came out of the anesthesia. He arranged for my dog to be there, too! That hospital Eucharist was the beginning of a recovery which was as spiritual as it was physical."

—John Smith
October 12 Ministry Minute speaker

We hope you heard John speak on Sunday! The Stewardship Campaign is going very well so far, and we appreciate your prayers.

Here is the good news:

- 28 families and individuals have pledged.
- 5 new pledges were received.
- 10 pledges increased from the previous year.
- 22% of the parish has pledged $34,000 to help meet the need for $154,000 for ministry in our parish.

Thank you! Please keep this ministry in your prayers and keep listening for stories of how God is changing lives through our church.

Participation Thermometer

Unlike secular fundraising organizations, churches do not tend to employ fundraising thermometers showing a financial goal (parish budget) with the red mercury-marker line that grows Sunday after Sunday as the community gets closer to its pledge goal.

There is, however, one very useful place for a thermometer: the percentage of the congregation's average Sunday attendance that has pledged. I call this a participation thermometer. In my last small parish, we simply used an enlarged pen and ink drawing of the chapel tower as the thermometer—it was the same image used throughout our campaign communications and as part of our parish logo.

In another parish we photographed a tall, thin church window and then used a common desktop photography program to convert the image into a black and white cartoon (this took two clicks and two seconds!). Then the image was enlarged and placed on foam core backing, and the children colored it in each Sunday with markers as involvement increased over time.

In both cases the image was placed by the sanctuary door. Each Sunday we figured what percentage of the total family pledging units had submitted their pledge, and we colored in the image to show the percentage change in involvement since the last Sunday. This encouraged those who had pledged because they saw a visual sign of their part in the stewardship campaign. This challenged the "not-yet pledgers" to get their pledge cards in. Above all, it emphasized participation rather than money.

A participation thermometer could easily be designed and created along with the case brochure, pledge card, case video and letter drafts six or eight months before the campaign even kicks off.

A Final Word on Cost, Speed and Creativity

What we know from nonprofit management about communications and marketing is this: you have to choose two out of the following three criteria for your project:

- Inexpensive
- Fast
- Beautiful, creative and well executed

In other words, you can always and only have campaign materials done . . .

- Inexpensively and fast, but not well
- Fast and well, but not inexpensively
- Inexpensively and well, but not fast

So be creative but do it well in advance, and thus take "fast" out of the equation and put "inexpensive" within reach. The clergy who tell me they simply do not have access to inexpensive creative design are usually hiding the reality that they procrastinated on the campaign management and are now up against a tight deadline. The truth is, in a church, a stewardship campaign is never, ever a surprise. Doing fearless fundraising requires doing well-planned fundraising. In the end, it really is that simple.

■■■■■■■■■■■■■■■■■■■■■■ ■■■■■■■■■■ ■■■■■■■■■■■■■■■■ ■■■■■

## CHAPTER 12

In the Thick of the Campaign

A frequent pitfall in campaign management is that, after the kick- off, everyone pulls in, on the one hand worried and fretting over how the job will be accomplished, on the other hand hiding under desks while they "hope for the best." Silence and avoidance are not management, nor are they faithful to our calling to lead.

The spiritual opposite to avoidance is enthusiasm, and the *dynamos* (energy) exhibited in the body of Christ is a gift of the Holy Spirit. A solid and maintained spiritual life will militate against procrastination and avoidance. This is why the quality of the leaders' spiritual life is so essential to fearless fundraising.

Spiritually centered, balanced leaders need to step up to carefully tend the campaign day by day, week by week, ensuring that communications and event-planning are on track to support campaign momentum. In this chapter, we will see the way a well managed and fearless campaign flows, from week to week, from save-the-date card to campaign-close evaluation.

RESOURCE

Model Campaign Schedule

Pre-Campaign

Five-point communications plan is implemented to get all members of the community to attend the Kickoff Event

1. Save-the-date cards	May
2. Invitation letter	June
3. Reminder postcard	July
4. Event invitation	Monday after Labor Day
5. Reminder postcard	Two weeks before event

Campaign Kickoff

1. Campaign Kickoff Celebration	Last Saturday in September
2. Kickoff Sunday Liturgy	1st Sunday in October
3. Mail pledge cards to those who did not retrieve one at the kickoff	Monday after kickoff

Campaign: Week One

1. Ministry Minute #1	2nd Sunday in October
2. Mail Ministry Minute flyer #1	Monday following 2nd Sunday

Campaign: Week Two

1. Ministry Minute #2	3nd Sunday in October
2. Mail Ministry Minute flyer #2	Monday following 3rd Sunday
3. Send invitation to Victory Celebration and begin turnout effort	Throughout week

Campaign: Week Three

1. Ministry Minute #3	4th Sunday in October
2. Mail Ministry Minute flyer #3	Monday following 4th Sunday

Campaign: Week Four

1. Ministry Minute #4	1st Sunday in November
2. Mail Ministry Minute flyer #4	Monday following 1st Sunday
3. Mail reminder cards and make phone calls for Victory Celebration	Throughout week

Campaign: Week Five

1. Ministry Minute #5	2nd Sunday in November
2. Mail Ministry Minute flyer #5	Monday following 2nd Sunday

Campaign: Week Six

1. Ministry Minute #6	3rd Sunday in November
2. Mail Ministry Minute flyer #6	Monday following 3rd Sunday

Campaign Closing

1. Victory Celebration	Last Saturday in November
2. Send thank-yous	
3. Evaluate campaign	
4. Begin planning for next year's campaign	

As you manage these steps, keep these points in mind:

1. *You are running a series of mini-campaigns*
Leaders should treat the Campaign Kickoff and the Celebration as a mini-campaign, working to get every person on the membership list to both events. Keep three lists on hand and updated: attending, non-attending, not-yet-responded—then focus on "not-yet-responded."

2. *Thank people early and often*
Thank-you notes should be sent to all those attending the kickoff—usually handwritten by the committee members or a group of volunteers. People love to be thanked for attending something important; the moment is also a fine teaching opportunity about the campaign's importance to the life of the community.

3. *Don't be afraid to ask inactive members*
Non-attendees—the people on the mailing list who are not part of the regular Sunday worshipping community—amount to about half the mailing list in most churches. These people have a relationship to the parish and should receive a pledge card in the mail, but a church leader should write a handwritten note at the end of the form letter, asking after their wellbeing and thanking them for considering a pledge to the campaign.

There is no harm in asking people to share their time and money with the church. Here is one of many situations in which stewardship and evangelism overlap. The worst that can happen is that 2 percent will ask to be removed from the mailing list, usually because of a move or a death, all of which is part of maintaining a well-managed mailing list.

Keep communicating!
Use telephone, e-mail, mailings, social media and the web—all these will help you to keep energy high. Do not withdraw, even if you are afraid you might not be meeting your goals or people may not be engaged. Silence is deadly in active campaign mode.

Mid-Campaign Check-ins

After about three weeks of Ministry Minutes, stewardship preaching, Christian formation programs on giving and a Rule of Life, bulletin inserts and/or campaign update flyers and web updates, you will find yourself mid-campaign.

This can be a scary time because it feels like the dull eye of the storm, the silence before the flurry of pledge cards in the final two weeks prior to the Victory Celebration party. So remain calm. Pray. Remember that God is working. Stay focused on the most important and not the most urgent tasks. Work your plan. Adjust your plan.

As the campaign progresses, do not fall to the temptation to avoid looking at the numbers. Pay attention to vital statistics like number of pledges, average Sunday attendance, number of new pledges, number of reduced pledges. Avoiding these statistics is a form of resistance, and the campaign leadership need to know the facts so that communication is open and adjustments can be made. In a worst case scenario, if pledges are coming in low or slow, postpone the Victory Celebration.

Weekly Checklist for Campaign Leaders

1. Pray for the campaign, those helping and those making their pledges

2. Be in touch with leaders and church staff

3. Create spreadsheet updating numbers relevant to campaign

   a. Number of pledges made to date (not counting verbal pledges)

   b. Percentage of active members (or ASA [Average Sunday attendance]) who have pledged

   c. Number of non-pledgers who are active in the community

   d. Number of non-active members who pledged due to campaign efforts

   e. Number of new pledges

   f. Number of pledge amounts increased from last year

   g. Number of pledge amounts decreased from last year

   h. Number who attended the campaign Kickoff Celebration

   i. Percentage of attendees as percentage of active members

4. Be in touch with people planning the Victory Celebration

5. Be sure that Sunday bulletins have fresh mentions of the campaign each week

6. Confirm the Ministry Minute speaker

7. Confirm that the Monday flyer is ready and only needs statistics to be inserted after collections on Sunday afternoon.

8. Check on the clergy person's engagement. Do they need anything for Sunday's announcements?

9. Update participation thermometer

10. Follow up with anyone who has indicated a desire to discuss planned giving, a major gift or other stewardship-related matter

To stay on top of all these details, the Stewardship Committee should meet weekly and, if yours is a small church with one or two campaign leaders, then the committee should meet with the clergy and the head of the lay leadership body (in most Episcopal circles, the warden). Good leaders are often busy, but these meetings can be done in person or using free conference calling services or free Internet video conferencing like Skype or Facetime.

Here is a sample of the weekly mid-campaign meeting agenda:

RESOURCE

Weekly Stewardship Ministry Meeting Agenda

1. Welcome and thanks

2. Prayer

3. Opening Report

4. Review of next week's initiatives:

    a. Theological content (sermons, forums, classes)

    b. Bulletin insert

    c. Weekly mailing

    d. Ministry Minute
       i. Name of speaker
       ii. Name of committee representative who will handle support for speaker

5. Plans for Victory Celebration

    a. How are RSVP's coming in? Do we need to make calls?

    b. How is event planning moving?

6. Phone-a-thon

    a. Will we need to call non-pledgers the final week before the Victory Celebration? Who will call and who will need to be called?

b. Review plan for the phone-a-thon, which was made in the spring
   i. Location
   ii. Food
   iii. Fun

7. Clergy person's thank-you notes

  a. Supplies in place

  b. Envelopes stamped and hand-addressed, ideally by a home-bound volunteer with plenty of time

  c. Has the clergy person set aside time and an ideal location to write thank-you notes?

8. Report to the vestry

  a. The report will be e-mailed to them in their vestry agenda packet, in time for careful consideration

  b. Live report to the Vestry during their meeting (Note: In most small churches, the vestry is made up of many if not all the Stewardship Campaign Committee—or at least there is substantial overlap. Regardless, every vestry meeting needs to have a "Stewardship" or "Financial Development/Stewardship" agenda item and live reports and discussion held in those meetings. Avoidance of the topic in vestry meetings is a form of resistance and is not only poor leadership but dangerous to the success of the ministry.)

9. Other business

10. Prayer

■ ■

These meetings will help you to stay on top of details. They will also keep you focused on your goal: to secure pledge cards from everyone who attends regularly, to conduct a series of successful Ministry Minutes, and to get 25 to 50 percent of those who do not attend regularly to pledge something.

That last task—converting non-pledgers to pledgers—is an essential task of any campaign. Some people are hesitant to make the shift, and they definitely have their reasons. You can address them throughout the course of the campaign.

Tips on Converting Non–Pledgers to Pledgers

Common reasons not to pledge	Suggested responses
"I don't want to make the commitment. You will get my money, but it will come in the plate as cash."	Remind the person that, just as a household plans expenses based on each month's salary, the church needs to plan based on what it expects to receive.
"I am not really the pledging type. I prefer you call me if you need something, and I will go buy it for the church."	Help the person to see giving as a gift and pledging as part of how we trust and support this community we call "church."
"I do not want to commit to a certain amount in case I incur financial problems later."	Each pledge card should have a clause (rarely used) regarding adjustment of pledges in the event of financial hardship.
"I do not want to commit to a pledge in case I get angry or disagree with something the church does."	Pledging is about right relationship with God and should not be primarily dependent on what the church does or does not do. If a person has a protest, they can pledge and then work for change.
"I don't like the rector (or the organist, children's minister, etc.)."	Just as we cannot bring a bottle of wine to a dinner party with a tag indicating who we think should drink it, we cannot designate the person who will benefit from our pledge. Giving is about God and not about who we do and do not like in church.
"I give at the end of the calendar year so that I know exactly what I can afford based on my real income."	If the person's income is based on sales, this is a fair need. In that case suggest that they pledge according to a fiscal calendar instead. They might also base a pledge on last year's earnings, and then adjust if necessary.
"It's an interim period, so I am not pledging until we find a rector."	Actually, an able candidate will look at pledging as one of the indicators of the health of the community. Strong pledging is essential to attracting healthy, able and effective clergy leadership.

Final Weeks of the Campaign

The Phone-a-thon

Why do we do phone-a-thons? It is true that most people prefer not to get calls at home and in the evening. It is also true that many people (this author included) do not even have landline phones, and some even keep cell phones in the car at night to protect against unwanted work-related calls.

But this call is different from a solicitation about the local newspaper or Tupperware. Being a member of a church is being a part of a community, and when you are a part of a community, you contribute to its life physically, prayerfully and financially.

All that said, people hate making these calls. So rather than send lists to volunteers and trust they will make campaign calls, host a phone-a-thon for a group to make calls in one night. Even if all but five people have pledged, host a phone-a-thon and call to invite those people to pledge.

Imagine you are in a small church, and only four people are on the Campaign Committee. That group of four could call the twenty-eight non-pledging families by all calling from their homes on the same night, and then gather at one person's house for dinner and the chance to commiserate about how hard it is. I prefer to locate a local business or large church office with multiple phone lines, and ask if we can use the space after hours.

You may not reach people or may not get returned e-mails, but the reminder is essential to move people to pledge and keep campaign energy high. In a society like ours, this support is actually a form of pastoral care.

So please do not shrink from calling members to ask for their pledge, and be sure to do it before the end of the campaign. Eighty-five percent of those who do not pledge before the end of the campaign will not pledge at all. Once the Victory Celebration is over, the air has left the balloon. The campaign will not re-inflate—especially if it failed to raise the money needed.

If you cannot reach a person, leave a detailed message along the same lines as the script below. E-mail reminders are also very valuable in addition to—but not as a substitute for—the calls.

Script: Last Year But Unfortunately Not This Year (or "LYBUNT")

Things to keep in mind:

1. Pray about the calls. The Holy Spirit is tender towards the people you are calling and towards you, the caller. The Holy Spirit knows how hard it is to talk about money. She will give you the words you will need when you need them, and She will help the person you are calling to hear you clearly.

2. Do not be afraid. Your ministry is helping people to let go of their death-grip on money. You are just facilitating what God is doing, and the people you are helping will feel good when they have given.

3. Be a good listener. In our nervous energy, we sometimes barrel through these conversations trying to get them over with. But this is a holy conversation. Let it flow and realize that if you are calm and sound peaceful, then they will respond that way.

4. Write notes from the conversation (with CONFIDENTIAL on the top of the page) that will help the pastoral leader (ideally the rector) to know how to better serve the people with whom you are speaking.

5. Have a stack of pledge cards, envelopes, pen and note paper with you. Each household you call should have a mailing label or at least a ready address so that you can write them a quick note and mail them a second pledge card as soon as you hang up. Do not go on to the next call until you have sent a note of thanks or a note with a pledge card. You should not underestimate how much people appreciate handwritten notes in an e-mail-based society. They work and they are appreciated.

6. Plan on about ten minutes per call: making the call and composing the handwritten thank-you note immediately after the call or the handwritten note in the event of a missed call with message left.

Possible script:

Hello, I am sorry to interrupt your evening but may I speak to _____?

(Make sure you have the name right; if the person goes by a nickname or middle name, you should know in advance.)

I am calling on behalf of _____ Church to follow up as we near the end of our Stewardship Campaign. It is going very well.

(Add a piece of good news, such as, "We are ahead of where we were this time last year, and people are on average increasing their pledges by more than __ percent!")

You pledged last year and we were hoping you could participate again this year. We would like to have all the pledges in by _____ so that we can form a ministry budget for our church. We hope to celebrate full participation of the whole church community at the ending celebration.

Would you like me to send you another pledge card? I have one right here I could drop in the mail to you.

Thank you for your time. Again, I am sorry to interrupt your evening but we are all committed to a strong and healthy church, and the budget and our pledges are part of that health.

Thank you. Good bye.

■ ■

At any point in the call, the responder may interject. You should stop, listen and graciously respond as factually as you can, but always try to get back to where you are in your script so that you get to the end.

If the person asks a question you cannot answer or if they express their anxiety by being cranky (some will, and it may have nothing at all to do with you or even your call), then just listen and ask if they would like the clergy person to call them back for a conversation.

Handwritten, Post Phone-a-Thon Note

Dear Sarah,

I was so glad to speak with you tonight. We very much appreciate your pledge to the St. John's campaign this year. Enclosed is another pledge card. I hope you will join us on the 25th for the Campaign Victory Celebration.

Warmly,
Charles

Dear John,

You will have received my phone message about the St. John's Pledge Campaign. I have enclosed a pledge card in case you need one as you discern your pledge this year. I hope you will join us on the 25th for the Victory Celebration—it will be a blast!

Warmly,
Sarah

Script: Prior Year But Unfortunately Not This Year (or "PYBUNT")

For those calling congregants who did pledge in past years but did not pledge this year (past year but not this year—PYBUNT)

Things to keep in mind when calling:

1. Follow same advice as provided for the LYBUNT calls.

2. Gather advance information: When was the last time they pledged? Were they regular? Was there a problem you should know about before you call (for instance, they are furious at the last rector or they lost their employment last year or they are upset with some aspect of church life). What you are told in preparation for the conversation is confidential and should be forgotten.

Possible script for the call:

Hello, I am sorry to interrupt your evening but may I speak to _____?

(Make sure you have the name right; if the person goes by a nickname or middle name, you should know in advance.)

I am calling on behalf of _____ Church to follow up as we near the end of our Stewardship Campaign. It is going very well.

(Add a piece of good news, such as, "We are ahead of where we were this time last year, and people are on average increasing their pledges by more than __ percent!")

We hope you will choose to participate this year. We are also hoping to have all the pledges in by _____ so that we can form a ministry budget for the church.

Would you like me to send you another pledge card? I have one right here I could drop in the mail to you.

Thank you for your time. Again, I am sorry to interrupt your evening but we are all committed to a strong and healthy church, and the budget and our pledges are part of that health.

Thank you. Good bye.

You can consult the "LYBUNT" script for tips on handling questions and for suggested post-call thank-you notes.

■ ■

The Final Sunday

The final Sunday of the campaign is what some call the "pledge card in-gathering Sunday." If you are celebrating the final Sunday with a festival liturgy and party to follow, you might follow this plan for the day:

- Avoid the temptation to have congregants fill out pledge cards while they are in church. The decision to pledge should come as a result of prayer, talk with family, reflection on budget—it should come in discernment and not in reaction.
- Have a clear area for people to hand in their pledge cards prior to worship, or finally in the offering baskets. Ushers should bring *all* pledge cards (those offered earlier in the campaign and those brought in this day) to the altar with the plate offerings.
- Thank people for pledging in creative ways throughout the service—during the Prayers of the People but at other moments, as well.
- Feel free to truly depart from the routine in your liturgical planning. A fall campaign might call for giving people apples, gourds, dried corn, small pumpkins and hay as they enter the church. After the blessing of the pledge cards, the people—young and old—could move to the altar during an anthem and place their apples and other signs of bounty in baskets and on the altar itself. Kids LOVE this and learn from it.
- If you are conducting an Advent campaign, you might decorate an Advent tree with purple ornament balls, adding one as each pledge comes in. The kids love to be invited up to place these ornaments, and the adults need to see that the campaign, week by week, is garnering new pledges.

Victory Celebration

Some communities think it is inappropriate to hold a Victory Celebration party following the festive service. Do not be tempted to forego the party! First of all, if there is no campaign-ending party, then pledge cards will drift in over the four months following the campaign— a disaster for planning and morale. Just as importantly, people have pledged a lot of money and deserve to be thanked and brought together for a party.

The gathering need not be (indeed should not be) extravagant but it can just as easily be enjoyable, fun and tasty. Get people who enjoy planning parties and set them loose: costumes, funny awards, skits, gag gifts, meaningful souvenirs such as a lovely icon book mark or a prayer card with a thanksgiving prayer—these items will cost pennies per person but serve as important tokens of gratitude.

It is best to host the Victory Celebration one of the weeknights following the final Sunday of the campaign. This way, most pledges come in on Sunday, but you still have a few days to get those final calls made and receive those final pledge cards before the party the following Friday or Saturday night.

Often churches tell me that "People won't come to a party for stewardship—they are too busy!" Again, I remind them that if the party is imaginative and thrown by a person well-known for being a great host, then people will come. They only avoid dull parties, which is why some of our churches need to be . . . well, a bit more fun.

For more on planning truly fun church events, see the section on "Special Events" in Chapter 9.

Stewardship Campaign Follow-up

Report Sunday is the week after the Victory Celebration and two weeks after the final Sunday of the campaign. To wrap up well, you want to manage these moments:

- Thank the membership, once again, for their hard work and generosity, and celebrate successes. This is a time for encouragement and not for scolding. I have seen a children's choir sing "Thank you, thank you, thank you" over and over to the "Happy Birthday" tune to great applause, so keep it simple and meaningful.
- Thank the committee and all those who helped manage the special events (Kickoff and Victory Celebrations). Thank-you posters and cards done by kids are always a huge hit. Get the children to draw a thank-you card and then color copy the drawings to make a series of cards. One drawing could be one side of the stewardship bulletin insert.
- Create a stewardship bulletin insert and use it to tell the congregation about the Stewardship Campaign, including
  1. Percentage of the membership who made pledges
  2. Average pledge
  3. Total amount pledged
  4. Increase of average pledge over last year's campaign
  5. Increase of percentage of parishioners who pledged
  6. Number of parishioners who attended the Kickoff and Victory Celebrations
  7. Any celebratory news about the campaign

Money is not an evil thing. Money is simply a tool. In a church, money is used to extend the ministry of God through each of us, to the lost, to the least, to the whole world. Discussing money in church, even putting information about money in the Sunday bulletin, is no more or less "holy" than discussing water or wine or electricity or prayer books.

Report Sunday brings money out of the closet and into the chancel. Celebrate life together—including the financial life of the church.

The "Thank You" Process

Within two weeks of the campaign, the vestry writes and signs an open letter thanking the church for the hard work, prayer, discernment and sacrifices, and (hopefully) reports that pledges have met the needs of the parish as discerned for the ministry budget of the next year (after which there is much rejoicing in the land).

The rector or lead clergy person takes a few working days of quiet (Advent, the liturgical season that begins just after Thanksgiving, is the perfect time to reflect after the close of a fall campaign.) During this time, he or she can write thank-you notes expressing gratitude to those who have pledged.

This personal touch is physically hard on the hand if your church has more than sixty families (I wrote three hundred annually in my last parish, but I spread it out over a week), but the benefit is incalculable. People like to be thanked personally, and they consider it an especially generous act on the part of their rector.

Tips for the Pledge Acknowledgement Process

Each pledger/donor needs to receive the following acknowledgement of their pledge and gift:

1. The party thrown for them at the end of the campaign

2. The verbal "thank you" on the final Sunday

3. A handwritten thank-you note from the rector, including the amount of money pledged

4. A formal letter of thanks from the treasurer, confirming pledge payment plans indicated on the pledge certificate

5. Reminder letters as needed for payment schedules, always in the form of a thank-you letter and never in the form of a bill, invoice or payment-due letter

6. A year-end thank-you letter on December 15, to be used for tax purposes, that notes what was received and that no services or products were provided for this payment

7. A phone call, if they indicated interest in discussing planned giving or a bequest

It is worth reiterating that clergy should know what congregants are pledging. If this level of trust and transparency is new to your congregation, then step in carefully. I promise you will enjoy seeing the way this openness removes the stigma and secrecy that so often surround money in our society.

If you are in any way concerned that the current treasurer is not trustworthy, is incapable of holding confidentiality, is controlling or will not participate in the thank-you process, then the current treasurer should consider a new ministry. Similarly, if the treasurer has a reputation for being untrustworthy or cantankerous, then a replacement in that job will greatly enhance the stewardship program.

Passing the Torch

It is recommended that the chairperson keep a notebook with samples, handouts, all minutes of meetings, notes, e-mails, commentary on activities and notes on how the program can be improved next year. An easy way to facilitate this process is to keep margins on the right side of all minutes quite wide, so that handwritten notes can be added.

This notebook should be passed to the rising chair when leadership changes hands. There is no reason for each chair to reinvent the wheel each year. A copy should also be given to the rector.

One of the final tasks for the outgoing team is to designate the next chair (again, usually this person was already serving as a rising chair), the rest of the stewardship leadership team, and a basic schedule for next year's campaign. They should take special care to set the dates of campaign kickoff and close, so that other dates and events can be planned around them.

Campaign Evaluation

The stewardship chair may want to collapse after the last table and chairs have been stacked at the close of the Victory Celebration dinner and indeed, if good work was done, then a rest is in order. However, a review of the campaign is immeasurably valuable not only to the next chair or the next team but also as a way to truly feel the "job well done," which is so deserved and so often left unheard in our American haste to get to the next thing.

The driving questions in an evaluation are these: "What went well? What did not go well? What would we do differently next time?" Answering those questions will take one meeting of the Stewardship Ministry Committee and one meeting of the stewardship committee chair with the vestry. In the case of a small church, this is simply a matter of devoting half of a vestry meeting to the evaluation conversation with the chair, who is usually a member of the vestry already.

The evaluation that follows is a simple but indispensable way to capture this information. These five pages should be placed as the last item in this past year's campaign manual, and at the front of next year's campaign manual.

Stewardship Campaign Evaluation

Church:_____ Chair:_____

Rector:_____ Rising Chair:_____

Committee names:_____

Date: (kick-off through Victory Celebration):_____

	2 years ago	last year	this year
Avg. Sun Attendance (ASA)	_____	_____	_____
Number of pledges	_____	_____	_____
% of ASA who pledged	_____	_____	_____
Average pledge	_____	_____	_____
# Converted non-pledgers	_____	_____	_____
# New pledgers	_____	_____	_____
# increased pledge	_____	_____	_____
# decreased pledge	_____	_____	_____
# non-pledging ASA members	_____	_____	_____
# non-pledging/non-attending	_____	_____	_____
# attended kickoff	_____	_____	_____
# attended victory	_____	_____	_____
# phoneathon calls made	_____	_____	_____
# new planned gifts announced	_____	_____	_____
# planned gift info requests	_____	_____	_____
# major gift asks (annual)	_____	_____	_____
# major gifts received	_____	_____	_____
# "Wish List" add-ons	_____	_____	_____
# thank-you notes sent	_____	_____	_____

Campaign Pre-planning:

What went well?

_____
_____
_____

What could have been improved?

_____
_____
_____

What would you do differently?

_____
_____
_____

Kickoff event:

What went well?

_____
_____
_____

What could have been improved?

_____
_____
_____

What would you do differently?

_____
_____
_____

Ending event:

What went well?

_____

_____

_____

What could have been improved?

_____

_____

_____

What would you do differently?

_____

_____

_____

Case development and presentation/communication:

What went well?

_____

_____

_____

What could have been improved?

_____

_____

_____

What would you do differently?

_____

_____

_____

Logistics:

What went well?

_____
_____
_____

What could have been improved?

_____
_____
_____

What would you do differently?

_____
_____
_____

Planned Giving notification:

What went well?

_____
_____
_____

What could have been improved?

_____
_____
_____

What would you do differently?

_____
_____
_____

Campaign energy (food, fun, excitement, creativity, participation, innovation, etc.)

What went well?

_____
_____
_____

What could have been improved?

_____
_____
_____

What would you do differently?

_____
_____
_____

(Attach samples of logo art or other identity standards used in the campaign.)

Other notes:

_____
_____

Next steps:

Leadership Changes:_____

Next Year's Campaign Committee to be convened: Date_____

Convener_____

Next Year's Calendar Prep-work:

1. Plan Completed
    Deadline:_____ Person Responsible:_____
2. Events on calendar/ dates published
    Deadline:_____ Person Responsible:_____
3. Case and financial needs set:
    Deadline:_____ Person Responsible:_____
4. Leadership recruited:
    Deadline:_____ Person Responsible:_____

Stewardship Questionnaires

Leaders may be tempted to issue a stewardship questionnaire. However, given the quality and quantity of resistance surrounding money in our church and culture, I suggest that *if* you ask for feedback, you ask carefully.

For instance, you are not served by open-ended questions like, "Did you like the stewardship program this year?" or "What can we do differently next year to improve stewardship ministry?" Since the work is essential both for the program of the church and the spiritual well-being of the members, questions such as these might be more helpful to gather people's thoughts and feelings following a campaign:

Stewardship Congregational Questionnaire

What did you most enjoy about this year's stewardship program?

How could we have improved on the Stewardship Campaign Kickoff Dinner?

How could we have improved on the Stewardship Campaign Ending/Victory Dinner?

What do you believe might improve the stewardship ministry and campaign?

■■■

By the end of a campaign, people have poured huge amounts of energy and money into their church. It is good to thank them and thank God, and it is important to learn from the experience and listen to people so that the ministry only grows stronger—and people become more fearless and generous—from year to year.

CHAPTER 13

■■■

The Major Gift

In any stewardship program—regardless of whether the congre-gation is twenty souls or two thousand, no matter what socio-economic situation the church is in and no matter how financially poor or wealthy the zip codes from which the congregation is drawn—there will always be people from whom a major gift needs to be asked.

Most major gifts fall somewhere between capital pledges and the bulk of annual pledges. A major gift can be asked for or simply offered. It can be for a specific thing or it can be undesignated. It can be for a specific purpose or it can simply be a very large annual Stewardship Campaign gift. It can be in honor of a person or an event or for a specific reason such as a new stained-glass window or a new furnace when the old one dies.

Major gifts are often given out of assets rather than income, except among the wealthy. These gifts also may come out of a bonus, an inheritance or reallocated savings.

Major gifts are not always massive gifts like the three-year pledges of a capital campaign, nor are they usually the pledges we make out of our regular income as a symbol that we understand that God is the giver of all we have. And yet, some of the gifts given in the course of an annual stewardship campaign are indeed "major gifts" and are asked for just as one would a "major gift."

The givers of major gifts generally enjoy giving the gift and once the askers have had their first experience, they become intoxicated by the joy of helping people to give to things they love and find meaningful.

Asking for a major gift often happens in capital campaigns and planned giving programs but it can happen at any time. I recently spoke to a suburban rector who received a $10 million pledge simply because he asked for it one day over lunch and had a very compelling idea as to what the $100,000 annually earned by that gift would do in his town to improve the lives of poor people. If he had not asked for that gift, then the local hospital or YMCA or animal rights organization would have.

If your congregation has twenty families, of which five are just making ends meet, fourteen are maintaining a solid but low income and can pledge the average annual campaign gift (about $1,100-$1,800), and you have one person who recently inherited his uncle's savings account of $40,000, then that person could give a major gift to the church if he or she so chooses and should be asked.

But asking for a $4,000 or a $40,000 gift for a church with an annual budget of $85,000 takes careful planning and conversation with the donor to get the gift right. That conversation is itself a gift, for both the church and for the donor. It also requires facing huge fears.

The Fear of the Major Gift

Occasionally I find a clergy person or warden who looks me straight in the eye and says no such people exist in their congregation. Saying there are no major gifts in your area is a way of avoiding the hard work of fundraising. Even the pastor in a hospital with a dying patient needs to be able to speak lovingly and intelligently if that person wants to discuss giving away their estate when they die.

Of all the discussions of money, asking for major gifts is by far the most laden with hesitation, fear and anxiety. The probability that Jesus' ministry was funded by women from whom Jesus or others asked major financial gifts seems to make no difference—we remain distinctly uncomfortable asking for money in the context of church and community life.

In many cases, including the annual Stewardship Campaign, there are some gifts so large or in need of such care that an individual request is need-ed. The fact is, there are some people—including some of us—who can and will make big gifts. Church leaders must consider how to have this conversation. Not dealing with those who can give major gifts is a kind of spiritual reverse discrimination, sometimes borne of undiagnosed envy and even anger that we do not have the money ourselves.

They say that the best way to get over a fear of horseback riding is to get onto a horse. The best way to get over the fear of asking for a gift (a gift that will bless the giver, bless the receiver and honor God) is to go ahead and ask for one. You will love how you feel when it is given! And you will love how you feel when you see the major donor's joy about giving it.

What Is a Major Gift?

In fundraiser's terms, a "major gift" is 1 to 10 percent or more of the total amount of gifts to the annual stewardship program of a church or ½ to 1 percent or more of the total amount of gifts to a capital campaign.

There are three kinds of major gifts:

- **Annual**: large, challenge or in-kind gifts to the church's annual budget
- **Special/Capital**: large gifts to a capital campaign that amount to three to twenty times the amount normally pledged to the annual Stewardship Campaign
- **Ultimate**: a gift of massive quantity or a planned gift through an estate

Major gifts usually are made in response to either a capital campaign, a special need or as part of an estate plan at death. Apart from those circumstances, major gifts come when you live in expectation of bounty rather than a pessimistic assumption of scarcity. If churches do not receive major gifts, it is because no one asks for major gifts, and *not* because major gifts do not exist in the congregation. Every pledger and every non-pledger is a prospective major gift giver.

Every Stewardship Campaign should be asking if any of those pledging should be on a short list of those whose gifts need to be personally solicited as a major gift. For more on how to manage that process, consider recruiting a fundraiser to your leadership team. They know a truly successful campaign depends on major gifts.

The Process Behind Major Gifts

As in any important ministry, there is a process and an art to asking for a major gift. The process generally includes the following steps:

- **Identification**: At this initial stage, we determine two things: what we will ask for and who could ask.
- **Qualification**: When it is time for qualification, we are separating the suspects from the prospects. A "**suspect**" is simply someone who has the ability to give but who is not involved or informed, and is unlikely to give to your campaign. A "**prospect**" is someone who has the ability to give a major gift and who also has the inclination to do so.

  A person or household becomes a prospect when we have done the hard work of informing and involving them so that they become someone with the relationships and the means to make a major gift. Do we know that this person can and is likely to give a major gift or is this just wishful thinking? Qualification comes from being both *able* to give a major gift and *inclined* to do so.

- **Strategy**: Do we have a plan? Best amount, best asker(s), best place, best literature to leave behind, best follow-up plan.
- **Relationship:** The relationship must be on both sides. There is no benefit (and possibly some harm) in asking a person for a major gift just because they live in a big house and come to church on Christmas Eve. There must be a free flow of experience and conversation back and forth, long before a gift is requested.
- **Request of the gift**: A specific amount needs to be asked for by the right person at the right time.
- **Acknowledgment**: Thanks needs to be planned out and managed properly.
- **Stewardship and renewal**: The results of the gift given by a major donor to the church must be communicated to the donor in such a way that they know their gift made a difference. They will then be more open to being asked again at some later time.

The Major Ask

Philanthropy has changed over the past few decades. In generations past, major gifts were only solicited during big capital campaigns that occurred every ten or twenty years. Today, major gifts are increasingly a part of annual fundraising, just as they have always been a part of planned giving.

I find that massive capital campaigns are becoming extinct in exchange for ongoing major gift requests. Clergy, wardens and fundraisers in churches need to know how to effectively ask for a major gift. Here is a primer:

1. **Humility and courage (or, getting your head ready to ask for a gift)**
   To ask for anything—even for something on behalf of another or on behalf of an organization—is a humbling thing. The mark of "being financially poor" (as opposed to being culturally, morally, intellectually, environmentally or relationally poor) is standing in line and needing to receive something from a person who has what you do not have.

   We church folk are so often sensitive to class issues, and loathe to make anyone uncomfortable; we just *hope* people will give. Then we are confused or even upset when the local library receives a $10,000 gift from Mrs. Jones, one of our parishioners.

   We cannot have it both ways. Either we swallow our pride and begin to see asking for major gifts as a ministry that helps both the person who gives and the church that receives, or we must stand idly on the sideline and watch the gifts go to other organizations and fund other missions around us.

2. Strategy (or, good planning gets the gift)

Think again on Mrs. Jones and her $10,000 gift to the library. What did the library do? Chances are, they did the one thing the church did not: they came up with a plan.

- The library committee sat and discussed members' relationships and who could make a large gift.
- They then spoke frankly about Mrs. Jones as a strong prospect.
- They did research to find out what she was passionate about, considering her family's history and the fact that she was a long-time teacher and loves children's literature.
- Then they sent the right people to ask: maybe an ex-pupil of Mrs. Jones who now is a teacher himself, along with Mrs. Jones's best friend, who has also pledged a gift of that same size to the library book fund.

The plan was not manipulative; it was just a well-organized request to which Mrs. Jones could say "yes" or "no."

3. Format (a written request versus a follow-up proposal)

It is so much easier to send a written request for a major gift—then we do not have to step into the vulnerability and humility of asking for the gift in person.

But think about your own perspective: would you rather a friend asked you for a favor in writing or in person and in the context of a conversation? Perhaps a letter to Bill Gates's foundation is required to receive a major gift from Mr. Gates, but our major gift requests in the church are friendship-based and need to be done in person, if at all possible.

Occasionally, a person may respond to a major gift request by thanking you for the visit and asking you to put the request in writing so that family may be consulted or so that the gift can be prayerfully considered, in which case an immediate and concise response within twenty-four hours is always best. You may even arrive with such a written request in hand in case they ask for it.

A written letter request or a proposal and cover letter should only follow a face-to-face request, never precede it. Fundraising is a human and relational endeavor, and major gifts fundraising even more so. Sending a proposal allows you to avoid face-to-face work, but it also removes the most wonderful, spirit-filled part of raising money, not to mention a distinct privilege for the fundraiser.

4. The Conversation (or, allowing for silence and the Holy Spirit)

There is no complexity to the conversation about a major gift. It *can* be emotionally and psychologically difficult if we try to do it based solely on our own strength. Remember that stewardship work is simply helping as the hands and feet of Christ. The Holy Spirit is in charge, and if not, then whatever we do will fail.

If you've covered that step, here are the others:

- **Preparation** is the most important part. Care has been taken to determine that the person being asked has both the ability to give the gift in question and the inclination to do so, based in their involvement in the project or organization along the way. The person being asked is already well-informed, tangibly involved and is therefore expecting—even waiting—to be asked. The interests of the person being asked are taken into consideration and an amount is predetermined.

  People are not offended when they are asked for too much, however they are offended if they are asked for too little. If you have asked for too much, the person being asked will simply make whatever gift they choose. If you ask for too little, then you are not only short-changing the church and its mission, but you are short-changing the donor as well.

- **Carefully choose the team who goes to ask for the gift**. Generally no more than three people go to make a major gift request, and one person—ideally a lay person—makes the ask, with the clergy person present if it is helpful. The person who asks for the major gift should be someone the donor likes and respects, who has given a gift of a similar size to the church at some time.

  Occasionally the clergy may be best positioned to ask for a large gift, but in general, I would argue that it is the people's church and not the priest's church. The rector can ask for the gift if he or she is giving or has given a gift at that level and does not feel there is emotional and pastoral power in play.

  While the priest may not be the best person to ask for the gift, he or she should be present because the donor is, in part, investing based on the clergy's leadership. It is appropriate for the rector to play a significant role in receiving the gift on behalf of the church.

- **The visit should be at the home or private office** of the person being asked and should be done at a time when no one is in a rush to get to the next place and no one is likely to be late. Restaurants and parishes are not good locations because they tend not to be private, and this kind of request is a very private event.

If you are concerned about planning a major gift request for people in different generations, there are several online resources that can help (go to www.churchpublishing.org/fearlesschurchfundraising and see the list of resources I have gathered). Making a misstep here can be detrimental to the receipt of the gift and to the ongoing relationship with the church.

For instance, elderly or infirm donor prospects—no matter how closely affiliated with the church and no matter how ready they seem to be to make a major gift or pledge—should be asked in the presence of a spouse, son or daughter or able relative or executor. This protects both the donor and the person(s) doing the asking.

- **Materials** to be given to the person being asked need not be complicated or voluminous. A stack of papers just complicates the conversation, overwhelms the donor and distracts the conversation—all of which can make the people asking seem defensive and confused. Anything the donor needs, such as a pledge card or brochure or set of building plans or letter proposal, can be left behind. Barring that, you can also mail the materials the next day. Never leave originals such as blueprints with a donor.

- **Come straight to the point**. Thank the person being visited for their time. Ask about the donor's schedule, so that the meeting does not end before you have asked for the gift. Review the project or issue for which the church is raising money. Note any recent large gifts received, if there are any, and then . . .

- **Ask for a specific amount**. People need to know what you are asking for. If you are worried about the request, then say something like, "We are asking you (and your family) to consider a gift of $5,000. This may be more than you were thinking about and it may be less than you were prepared to give, but this is what we are asking for."

- **Allow silence.** This is the most awkward and holy part of the conversation, and it is often where leaders get nervous, anxious and upset as they wait. Horrible doubts begin to run through your mind. Ignore the doubts, maintain dignity and composure, and wait for the person being asked to speak first.

  Silence does not mean discomfort or anger. In the silence, the Holy Spirit is working and the person being asked is thinking or even praying. Please do not interrupt that work of the Holy Spirit, which is an essential part of the discernment of the donor.

- **Relationship, relationship, relationship**. Remember that parish life is about relationships. These are often friends or at least regular acquaintances. Rely on the Holy Spirit to draw you near one another, and rely on your shared love for the church and community as the foundation of the conversation.

- **Be grateful**. If the pledge is lower than you had hoped, do not negotiate. Fall back and know that more work needs to be done to communicate the value of the organization prior to the next request.

The Ask on the Telephone

In some churches, the larger gifts of the annual Stewardship Campaign are asked for in face-to-face or telephone conversations as peer-to-peer solicitation. Telephone conversations may also be used in the clean-up phase or community phase of a capital campaign to raise the last 5 percent of funds.

Here are a few suggestions for a successful call:

Preparation:

1. Do not procrastinate. As soon as you have the names and numbers of people you are calling, make plans to make the call. Procrastination is the worst enemy of a campaign and especially of asking for gifts.
2. Be sure you are asking someone for a gift you are willing to give or have given. Your calls should only be made to peers in giving levels or to those giving less than you have given.
3. Make sure you have given your own pledge first and be clear to the prospective donor that you have done so.
4. Study the case for support (the document or video that explains the organization's vision, what the money will support, and why it is so important to make this gift now).
5. E-mail or call the donor to ask when you might make a call about the campaign. Set a telephone appointment that is convenient to the donor. Donors may want their spouses on the line, or they may have a time of day that best suits them. By making an appointment in advance, you are more likely to have a stable, unrushed conversation when both parties are able to relax, pray and be present to the moment.
6. Make the call from a phone that is guaranteed to have good reception. You should be seated in a building with the door closed and able to concentrate. Unstable cell reception, family background noise, office interruptions and rushed conversations because another (more important) call is waiting, or distracted conversation while driving or grocery shopping, are all recipes for disaster on a campaign call.
7. Plan to make the call on a Saturday morning if possible when everyone is well rested. An early evening, especially Sunday, is second best as a choice.

8. When making the call, have these items in front of you so you can easily answer the donor's questions in the midst of the conversation:
   a. The case for support
   b. The basic budget of the case for which the gift is being asked
   c. The giving history of the person being asked for a gift
   d. Your calendar, in case the donor requests another conversation or a meeting
   e. The deadlines and calendar of the campaign
   f. The status of the campaign (participation, amounts raised so far, etc.)
   g. The details of any upcoming campaign event this donor will be asked to attend
   h. A pad for taking notes, which you may or may not want to provide to the clergy or campaign chair or, in a large church, the development staff

The Call Itself:

Just before the call:

1. Make the call when the donor has asked you to make the call. Scheduled calls are the only way to be relatively sure of connecting. A major gift cannot be asked for in a message or in a series of phone-tag conversations—no matter how tempting that might be to the caller.
2. Ask those around you not to disturb you while on the call.
3. Turn off all other telephones or music.
4. Take a few minutes for absolute silence. If you are afraid, then light a candle to remind yourself of the real presence of the Holy Spirit. Say a prayer asking the Holy Spirit to inspire the conversation you are about to have and to fill the time with clarity of speech and hearing. Thank God for this person—for their ministry and for their membership in the community. Ask God to give you the wisdom to know what to say and when to remain silent.

As you make the call:

1. Take a deep breath and have a moment of silence to collect your thoughts and remain peaceful.
2. Thank the donor for his or her time.
3. Tell the donor why you are calling (even if the person knows).
4. Touch on the following topics:
   a. *"I have made my pledge."*
   b. *"We are seeking to accomplish . . ."* (summarize the case for support, perhaps using a text you have created or a three to six sentence summary provided by the campaign leaders)

c. *"I am asking you (and your partner, spouse, etc.) to consider a gift of $____ to the campaign. This may be more than you were thinking of giving and it may be less, but this is what I am asking you to consider."*

4. Hold and do not break the silence.

5. Listen carefully to the response, taking notes if you need them for later reference in the conversation (in general, you should destroy them after the call).

6. If you do not get a firm and definite response, then ask one of the following:

   a. *"Do you want a written proposal for the request? Would that help you in your consideration?"*

   b. *"Would you like to think, pray and reflect on this request? If so, when would you like me to call back?"*

   c. *"Is there anything else I can provide to support your decision-making?"*

   d. *"Would you like to meet face to face if you have other questions?"*

   e. *"When might we expect your pledge card? The deadline for this campaign is (insert date) and we are grateful for your participation in it."*

6. If you do get a firm and definite response:

   a. *"Is there anything else I can provide to support your decision-making?"*

   b. *"Would you like to meet face to face if you have other questions?"*

   c. *"When might we expect your pledge card? The deadline for this campaign is (insert date) and we are grateful for your participation in it."*

   d. *"Thank you for your time and consideration."*

After the call:

- Hand write a thank-you note.
- E-mail or call the campaign office or the church office to let them know the status of the campaign call.
- Destroy personal notes from the conversation or mark them confidential for the major gifts file you are creating on all major gifts prospects.
- Send any information you think should be conveyed to the church leadership, such as pastoral issues that need follow-up, disappointments expressed by the donor, etc. If mailing this material, mark it confidential.
- Make the next call.

Tips on Dealing with Voicemail

When calling to ask for a pledge, only leave a message asking when it is best to call back to set an appointment to have a conversation. Do not ask for the pledge in a recorded message. Leave a phone number, best times to reach you and an e-mail address. Keep calling until you get a live person for the conversation, even if you need to make four to six calls (the maximum). If you get no response, make note of what you accomplished and the response (or lack of one) and return the information to the campaign office or church office so that it can be given to a new caller.

Donor Recognition

There is an art to thanking people well, and every campaign should master it. There are a few things to consider as you design your recognition plan for the stewardship program:

1. The first "thank you" should come from the rector, vicar or priest-in-charge. It should:
   a. Be handwritten on attractive yet inexpensive card stock
   b. Be legible (if you have bad handwriting, then use a printer to craft the body of each note in an informal script; then hand write the salutation ("Dear _____ ") and the concluding signature ("Sincerely yours, _____") in ink
   c. Be sent out ideally within twenty-four hours of the receipt of the pledge or gift, and at the latest within thirty days of the end of the campaign
   d. Include the amount pledged for the year
   e. Be kept short (two or three sentences)

RESOURCE

Acknowledgement Letter from Clergy

Dear (first name[s]),

Thank you for your pledge of $_____ to the life and ministry of our church. Your gift back to God through this ministry will be carefully put to good use. On behalf of those whose lives will be touched by this gift, I am pleased to offer my thanks.

Warmly yours,

(Clergy first name)

2. The second communication should come from the treasurer and should:
   a. List the terms of the gift and its amount (frequency of payments, etc.)
   b. Note that payments will be acknowledged quarterly
   c. Note that a final tax acknowledgment will be sent in the first week of January
   d. Note that the gift amount is strictly confidential between the treasurer and the clergy person in charge of stewardship
   e. Be typed on church stationary, standard letter size, with a real inked signature
   f. Include no personal note
   g. Be stamped "confidential" with an ink stamp or as part of the printed letter

3. The acknowledgment of payments should be monthly or quarterly. Pledgers should never be unsure as to how they stand on their pledge payment unless they specifically request that no statement be provided regularly. It bears repeating that pledge payment reminders and acknowledgements should take the form of a mail-merge letter and never look like a bill or invoice.

Quarterly Acknowledgement Letter

December 31, 2012

Dear (*formal saluation*),

Thank you for your gift to (*church name*).

Your gift made possible the work we are doing through. . . (*insert specific comment related to the purpose for which the funds have been given*).

We have received your check # _____ (or "We have received your electronic payment) dated _____ in the amount of $_____.

No goods or services were provided in exchange for your donation. Once again, we thank you for your generous contribution.

Faithfully yours,

(Treasurer's signature in blue ink)

Cc: Treasurer

■ ■

4. Late payments should be solicited gently by a brief form note from the treasurer asking if there is anything the church can do to assist with payment. This letter should take the tone of a thank-you letter.

5. A tax acknowledgement should be sent from the treasurer to acknowledge all payments made prior to midnight December 31 or, in most situations, as late as four days into the new year. The letter should look like the quarterly note modeled above, except that it also includes the total giving for the year.

   NOTE: Donors may deduct contributions only in the year the gift was made:
   - Checks: the date on the check, not the post date
   - Credit card: the date of the transaction
   - Pay-by-phone: the date of the transaction
   - Properly endorsed stock certificates: the post date of the mailing
   - Electronic stock transfers: the date of the actual transfer from the corporation

Four Reasons People Don't Give a Major Gift

Sometimes, all your efforts are for naught and the gift just will not come. Here are some reasons, most of which you can address before they occur:

1. Lack of basic trust
Sometimes, the wrong person is sent to ask for the wrong gift at the wrong time from the wrong person. Giving a major gift is based on trust and connection. If there has been even a hint of financial or other mismanagement in the church, or if there is doubt in the church's leadership, then trust is compromised and a major gift will not be given.

2. Failure to demonstrate the inherent value of the parish's mission, vision and service
Generally, the most common reason people do not give a major gift is because they have not been convinced that the ministry is worthy of it. The case for support must be well communicated and compelling.

3. A sense of urgency is not communicated
When there is poor planning and/or poor communications, the sense of urgency—which inspires a person to make a major gift—is absent, and the gift is not made. People do not give to a program that does not seem to need their gift.

4. Negativity

No donor will give a major gift to a campaign under dire circumstances. If the request comes with a "sinking ship" message to save the drowning organization from financial disaster, then the pledge is doomed from the start. Take note: in economic downturn, the donors do not want to hear how the economic downturn is affecting your organization. They want to hear how your organization is helping people whose lives have been traumatized by economic downturn.

So build and nurture strong relationships, tell your story with confidence and urgency, and stay positive, and there is no reason your congregation will not receive the gift Mrs. Jones almost sent to the library.

## PART V

The Ripple Effect: Stewardship-Related Concerns

CHAPTER 14

■■

Planned Giving Programs

Planned giving is to fundraising what the hum of a refrigerator is to a busy household—there all the time, running quietly in the background.

Any American church without an ongoing planned giving program is not paying attention and is letting money that could secure its future hemorrhage to other nonprofits. The truth is this: organizing planned giving is like catching fish in a fishbowl, especially as the generations for whom church was essential get older and prepare to pass on their assets. Everyone, without exception, is going to die, and some will leave something behind that they would love to give to their church . . . but only if they are asked nicely.

Setting up a planned giving program takes about ten minutes and ten seconds. Here is an easy plan:

1. An intelligent person says to the vestry, "Our members are dying and leaving their estates to the YMCA. Let's have a planned giving program in our church!" (1 minute)
2. The vestry agrees. (10 seconds)
3. The announcement is made to the congregation the next Sunday that the church is now officially receiving planned gifts. (1 minute)
4. The following two samples are photocopied and distributed. (5 and 3 minutes, respectively)

From there, a clergy person should be able to manage follow-up, including:

1. Work with a team to draw up a wish list for the use of proceeds
2. Meet with members to discuss end-of-life issues
3. Manage a few targeted meetings with older members to ask for a planned (major) gift

---

Job Description for Planned Giving Contact Person

Term: Five or more hours per year

1. Create or secure planned giving brochures (for a sample, see www.churchpublishing.org/fearlesschurchfundraising)

2. Plan and manage a Planned Giving Sunday

3. Place occasional announcements in bulletins, on websites and in newsletters reminding people to make a planned gift

4. Ensure planned giving information is available on the church's website

5. Meet with the church's leadership team to urge them to prioritize planned giving

6. Produce and regularly update a list of those who have remembered the church in their estate plan (verbal communication also qualifies), and frame and post the list publicly in the church

7. Meet with the Rector or other Planned Giving Leader to set goals regarding visits to congregants/members asking them to remember the church in their estate plan. Follow up with them to encourage that they meet their visit goals. (A good starting number in a small church is one per month.)

Planned Giving Bulletin Insert

© Digit30, Dreamstime.com

How can I leave a gift to my church?

The largest financial gift any of us is likely to give is the one we plan for the end of our lifetime.

We are often hesitant to make planned gifts because it is difficult to imagine the time after our own death. And yet, we all know of a saint who left a gift that has provided for our church's life together. We are grateful to them for making that planned gift. Each of us has the same opportunity.

What is a planned gift?

There are two kinds of planned gifts: Outright (or current) gifts are transfers of cash or stock as part of an estate plan. Deferred gifts are given with special income arrangements such as bequests or annuities.

What is a bequest?

A provision made in one's will through which the parish receives cash or other assets at the time of the giver's death.

What is a charitable gift annuity?

A legal agreement between the giver and the parish through which the giver exchanges cash, stocks, or other assets for an agreed-upon income for life.

What is a charitable remainder trust?

Used to transfer assets to a trust which then goes to the parish after the last beneficiary dies. It also provides the giver a fixed or variable income for life.

What is a life estate contract?

Transfer of real property to a parish while reserving rights for you or others to live on the property for life. (Charitable deductions are limited to properties that are either personal homes or farms.)

What is a charitable lead trust?

Transfers assets to a trust, the income of which goes to the parish for a period of years while the assets revert to the donor or heir at the termination of that period.

■ ■

## CHAPTER 15

Capital Campaign Management

Whole books are written about capital campaign management, so I will offer a basic vocabulary here, mostly designed to take the fear out of this important fundraising ministry.

The Changing Tide

In earlier generations, capital campaigns were massive and rare thrusts of major giving, and they represented goals of ten to twenty times the value of the annual budget of a parish.

In the 1980s as the economy boomed and buildings boomed with it, all that changed. The resulting shift to smaller and more frequent capital campaigns is not something to like or to dislike. It is just the new now.

Another major change has hit capital giving: in the past, 80 percent of the gifts came from 20 percent of the people in our pews. Now 95 percent of the gifts come from 5 percent of the people. I fully expect that by the third decade of this century, as the gap between rich and poor widens, we may see 98 percent of major gifts coming from 2 percent of the congregation.

This change makes it imperative that two things happen in the management of capital campaigns. First, planning must at least in part focus on early and maintained communication with and involvement of those who will be giving the biggest gifts.

Second, a distinction between "**prospects**" and "**suspects**" must be carefully discerned and considered. See the major gifts discussion back in Chapter 13 for an explanation of these related but not synonymous categories.

Thinking and hoping that a suspect will make a huge gift to the capital campaign is not an act of faith, but rather an act of wishful thinking. Converting a person from suspect to prospect requires moving a suspect into the center of the life of the parish and the campaign planning process. Just because someone has a lot of money and goes to church, their name does not belong on the prospects list.

Preparing for the Campaign

The best way to prepare for a capital campaign is to follow a few simple rules:

1. Three effective years of annual stewardship campaign work is the best way to prepare for a major gifts or capital campaign.
2. Be ready for a somewhat counter-intuitive reality: about three-quarters of the time and energy should be devoted to planning and cultivation of the donors, while only the last one-quarter of the time and energy will be devoted to actually asking for and receiving the money.
3. If annual stewardship programs are well managed, and if the capital campaign planning, case development and cultivation phases are not rushed, then annual pledge fundraising should not in any way be harmed by a capital campaign and vice-versa. If anything, a well managed capital campaign will always increase annual pledge campaign strength.

   Consider a joint annual giving/capital campaign ask. For example, if Mrs. Jones consistently pledges $1,800 to the stewardship campaign, then ask her to maintain her annual pledge and to add a capital campaign pledge of $10,000 over five years. This would make her annual gift $3,800 a year for five years. At the end of the five years, when the capital pledge is paid, you could ask her to increase her $1,800 annual stewardship pledge to $2,500, since she has gotten used to a $3,800 annual payment.
4. Begin planning years before you ask for your first capital pledge and ask from the top down (biggest to smallest).
5. The more the major donors have been intricately involved in the designing of the campaign and the case, the more likely they will be to make a substantial gift.
6. The case needs to generate a response from the prospective donor. Aim for this:

   "Wow! We have all been planning for so long, and I can see some of my ideas here. This work needs to happen for the good of our community and our church. I am giving a huge gift, and it's about time they asked!"

and not

"*What a half-baked, empire-building, institutionally narcissistic project! I have heard little about this and suddenly they want me to pledge $50,000? I could give $100,000, but this campaign will get none of my support!*"

The Phases of a Capital Campaign

The Leadership Phase

Time: Entire campaign

In this phase, the clergy person meets quietly with the wardens (or the equivalent elected leaders), some of the church members most committed to the vision and some of the most financially well-resourced members. Together, they discuss a vision for a capital campaign and offer early input. Slowly, with this group's help, the clergy leader develops a list of three to six people who fit these criteria:

- The largest donors
- The most involved
- The most experience and the least resistance to stewardship

This list comprises the "leadership donors," and they are integral to the campaign's success. This phase is the most important in the campaign and runs through the entire period leading up to the public phase, which does not begin until as much as 90 percent of the money has been pledged with signed pledge forms from leadership donors.

The Discernment Phase

Time: Up to one month per $100,000 in the goal

The discernment phase is designed to provide an awareness of God's call on a church. This time of discernment and reflection—in tandem with study and input—is the firm foundation of any successful capital campaign. When the early stages of prayer, congregational involvement, study and communication are shortcut, then the entire campaign—and the church's future stability—may be in jeopardy.

The focus of the discernment phase is **prayer and involvement:** listening to the congregation and to God—for where God is calling the congregation, what new ministries or direction the Spirit is moving the community toward. How this prayer is encouraged is up to each individual church.

The Study Phase

Time: Up to one month per $100,000 in the goal

The study phase is designed to complement the discernment phase, honoring the input and the direction of the Holy Spirit while not neglecting the very important work of obtaining and considering data. In some situations, a vestry may be divided into two groups, one of which encourages discernment while the other manages study.

The study phase has two parts. The first part is external and the second part is internal. Generally speaking it is best to begin with a collection of external data, especially the local demographic trends. By starting with the external data, the church is encouraged to look outward before it looks inward. Internal data is eventually collected to make clear the use of the facilities on a day-to-day basis.

Once you have determined that what you are raising is truly capital development and not simply deferred maintenance (which should be paid for out of annual budgets from a deferred maintenance savings program), then you need to determine what the new facility will require. This work, if done well, takes time and patience but will pay off in the end. An abbreviated effort at this discernment will weaken the plans, the case and the campaign. Questions you might ask would include:

1. What new construction do we need to do and for what purpose?
2. How does this fit into our short- and long-range planning for the church as a whole? Is this part of a vision for fifty years or is this an effort to solve an immediate problem?

3. Who will be using those spaces and when?

4. Do these or other spaces have marketability during the week as commercial rental space?

5. What patterns of change are we seeing in planning for our town or city? Is the population aging or becoming younger?

6. Has site selection been carefully considered, especially in terms of other phases of building for future generations?

The same questions will inform the conversations and plans you make moving forward, including the detailed description of the space needs, which is usually drafted with an architect and as many intended users and major donors as possible. Then a budget is developed to represent the cost of these plans for capital development.

The Input Phase

Time: Can run concurrent with the study phase

The input phase is designed to elicit input from every person in the church, regardless of their expertise, experience, attendance or pledging level. Time spent in this phase accomplishes two important goals:

First and foremost, asking for input from the congregation makes people aware that the campaign is on the horizon, and invites them to be a part of the design of capital changes. Asking people to make a pledge without having truly engaged them by asking their opinion will not only reduce the likelihood of a pledge; it will likely offend the person from whom a pledge is being asked. To ignore the input phase of a capital campaign is effectively saying to a congregation, "We want your money but not your opinion."

This input can be collected in many different ways and is not dissimilar to the questionnaire suggested in the annual pledge campaign preparation. This is a key step to asking for money: ask for opinions first. This data collection and listening process can be done with questionnaires, dinner conversations, site tours and congregation-wide events. It should be done throughout the campaign in different phases of development and building so that donors feel included and feel that their opinions matter and have been requested.

Even as building takes place, hard-hat tours are a valuable way to add new input sessions—although input in dreaming and drawing phases are primary and essential. Some of the key questions you will be asking are:

1. What do you think we need to build?
2. How would you change our physical plant to better serve the future members of our church and the community?
3. To what extent does our building make possible our vision of ministry?
4. Who do you know who could help us with this?
5. If you could give $__ million, what would you build?
6. Who do you think could and would invest in this project?

The Public Phase

Time: Usually only a few weeks

The public phase of a capital campaign is designed to raise the final 5 to 10 percent of the campaign goal, which will come from 95 percent of the members. Though the amount may be small—most people give $1,000 to $6,000, distributed over three years—it is important that everyone be given the opportunity to make a pledge. The public phase of the campaign should be designed for inclusion rather than significant fundraising, communicating to members that every pledge and every person matters.

CHAPTER 16

Generational Sensitivity
and Strategy

Planning for the Generational Shift

Beginning in 2015 and progressing beyond, the baby boomer generation will begin to age out and will start to hand over both involvement and pledging in our churches to Generations X (those born between 1960 and 1980) and Y (those born between 1980 and 2000).

For the past 1,700 years, since the reign of the emperor Constantine, the church has enjoyed a season in which giving was the result either of fear, manipulation, taxation or affiliation. The World War II Generation (young adults during the Second World War) and the Silent Generation (people born just before or just after the Second World War) were the last two generations affected by these forces.

These anchor generations did not pass those strong ties on to their children in the baby boomer generation. And those boomers passed even less faith on to their children. As a result, Gen X, the eldest of whom turned fifty a few years before this book was published, will be the first generation for whom church attendance, involvement and pledging are not a given.

In other words, churches that do not start now to improve how they plan their mission, how they communicate their mission and how they ask for pledges to support their mission will find their budgets decimated and their doors closed within one to three decades.

Unlike their parents and past generations, Gen X-ers and Gen Y-ers have many options for social and spiritual connection and philanthropy—most of them online—making it all the more essential that churches involve them in leadership, include them in decisions about mission and ask them boldly and clearly for financial investment.

Getting to Know the Generations

While there is plenty of diversity within each generation, and generalizations are a dangerous business, certain characteristics have emerged regarding the way generations communicate, join groups, support church, like to be asked for money and give money away.

The World War II and Silent Generations were the last generations to give or attend the church because of these primary reasons:

- This is what my family has always done.
- This is what my "tribe" (people, ethnic group) does.
- Our church makes our town (village, community, neighborhood) a better, more stable place.
- Our church is trustworthy and trains our children in morals and good choice-making.
- Going to or giving to church makes one a good citizen.
- When I pay my bills with a check and assemble the envelopes to be mailed off, it is easy to add a check to the church on a monthly basis.
- Our clergy stop by often just to sit with us in the kitchen for a cup of coffee—they are like family to us.
- Making a gift to the church is the main way to make a contribution to a worthy cause.

What factors control the landscape now? Media, especially the Internet, have changed everything for generations coming to age in the latter twentieth and twenty-first centuries. The church has not yet awakened to the new face of philanthropy, which happens as much by "search and click, enter and click" as completing a pledge card and writing a check.

Instead, younger donors are likely increasingly independently minded and may think in these terms:

- I have endless opportunities to contribute to groups that support my passions. All I have to do is type "nonprofit" or "donation," plus a few key words like "planet" or "hospital" or "hungry children."
- I am suspicious of the institutional church and do not consider it automatically trustworthy.
- I do not carry a checkbook, nor can I find it easily at home.
- Rather than gather at the general store or block parties or even the front porch, I would rather gather with far-flung friends on Facebook or chat via text.
- It would be strange if a clergy person offered to stop by my small apartment. We have had a few cups of coffee and we are Facebook friends, but I would not say my priest "knows" me.

- A pledge card is not going to show up on my radar, but a Kickstarter Campaign on Facebook might.

Even though this book has detailed the technologies of pledge cards and campaigns, the reality is that we are the only institution still asking for pledges, communicating why people should give and receiving payments on pledges the way they did two generations ago. The people who are able and willing to give in that way to the church are now entering into their last phase of life. Their children, grandchildren and great-grandchildren are no longer moved by the church's reasons to give, no longer communicating the way the church is communicating and no longer pledging the way the church is asking them to pledge.

The Church Philanthropy Turning (CPT)

Younger people have different motivations for giving to the church and will give to the church in different ways. It is more than a demographic blip. I call the shift that is now underway the Church Philanthropy Turning (CPT).

This turning is the great reversal of power between donors and charities that began in the 1950s. In the days when people went to the faith community closest to their home, churches had a somewhat captive audience and thus a certain power. For centuries in the early phase of many Christian churches, membership at a certain church was mandated either by state religious laws (before the Industrial Revolution) or by civil laws (until Title VII of the Civil Rights Act of 1964 which had allowed employers to hire and fire based on religious affiliation). People were often not only forced to go to church but to a certain church. Freedom or at least income and social status depended on church membership. Churches could afford to be less transparent, less responsive to donor/pledger interests and less flexible in program and service provision. You paid your pledge, you got what you got, and you were expected not only to like it but to keep supporting it.

People under forty-five today will not object to back-room decision-making by clergy and vestries. They will not be upset by endless annual meetings that say little about the way money is being spent. No, Generations X and Y will not be bothered by these things . . . because they will simply un-fund such churches in favor of either a transparent, responsible program or a walk in the woods and some prayer with friends around a meal.

As one Gen X-er recently said to me at a coffee hour, "We do not need to do battle with misogyny, racism, waste or homophobia in our older generations of church leaders. We just have to live our lives and wait, while they get older and too tired to fight anymore. I give it about ten years."

That attitude might make it sound like young donors are withdrawn or stingy. Actually, the same young member told me she has no problem giving money. "I give because I must," she told me enthusiastically. "I must give because of all that God has given to me. Giving makes me joyful. Giving back to God by giving to the mission of the church is fundamental to my spiritual life. All I am saying is that, although I do not have much choice about *if* I give, I have tons of choice about *where* I give."

So how do you connect and help these young members not only to become generous but to share that generosity with the church? It helps to understand a few forces that shape their lives and worldview.

First of all, people under age forty-five make up almost 40 percent of the U.S. population. While they are a smaller percentage of the church, they have plenty of power outside of it. Those who have disposable income so young have earned their money and have not inherited it. Many are still paying off loans and raising children and most will not begin to reach peak giving for four more years, when they reach ages forty-nine to seventy.

Unlike their parents and even grandparents, they were not the children of people who saved, budgeted or planned the use of their money. And younger donors are not inclined to repeat the mistakes of their last two generations and are more than a little resentful of the situation in which their parents and grandparents have placed their planet.

Perhaps rather surprisingly, almost 30 percent of Americans with a net worth of one million dollars or more are under age forty-four. Most clergy and lay leaders will say, "We don't have any people under forty-four in our church with any money," but that is likely just not true.

Donor-Driven Mission versus Church-Driven Mission

Younger donors to our churches are often giving precisely to that—the mission. In their theory of church, they have returned to the age immediately after Jesus' day, when the church was a movement and not yet an institution. They are mission-driven donors, but make no mistake: they are driven by *their mission* and not the mission of the church.

Younger donors may be giving to the church out of a deep understanding of stewardship and gratitude. They may even be tithing, but they are much more inclined than past generations to give to the mission of their choosing. That passion can be the church's mission—or at least a part of it—but the church is not a given.

In other words, the days of members providing unquestioning funding for the mission of the church are over. Instead, we have the responsibility to meet the needs of these younger donors rather than having the donors meet the needs of the church.

That donor sensitivity is something secular nonprofits have mastered for decades. Thankfully, this change does not have to change the church's mission, because the church is not the institution or the buildings or the programs or even the worship. The church is the people of God living *inside* those buildings, attending those programs and worshiping their God.

Ten years ago, the question pledgers had to answer was "To which church shall I give my gift back to God?" Now the question is "What in the world needs funding and can I see my church doing that in some way, based on what they tell me about how they use my money? And if the church is not getting good work done, is there an organization that is? "

These young members may still come to church if the programs are enjoyable and the worship compelling. But they may not do more than drop $20 into the plate as it goes by—the value of an hour and a half of entertainment per week.

The advent of donor-driven giving is going to be very healthy and very challenging for our churches. Church budgets are going to increasingly become a conversation between church leaders and younger donors. If a parish can communicate effectively with their younger donors and make clear what the church is doing, why it is doing it, and how it is in keeping with Jesus' request that we "do this in remembrance of me," then all shall be well.

Young donors do not want the church to go away. They want to understand how what they see and experience on Sunday morning is connected to what they and their fellow Christians are accomplishing the rest of the week. But they have a well-honed sense for when someone is lying to them or talking down to them.

Another interesting thing to note about younger donors is that not only do they like to fund things that are a part of their mission on earth, they also tend to fund projects in which they are directly involved. The parents of Gen X (the Silent Generation) were content to write a check and sit rather passively in the pews while "Father so and so" worked on the budget and mission with his vestry. But Gen Y and Gen X donors like to be physically or at least logistically and emotionally engaged in the mission of the nonprofit to which they give.

That means the church has to engage them in mission both through regular communications and through presence-making beyond Sunday morning worship (though engaging and moving Sunday morning worship is a huge plus).

By involving younger donors in the life of the parish between Sundays (and yes, they *will* come if the invitation and event is attractive, fun, meaningful, full of interesting people and engaging), you are meeting younger donors on the field, making it much easier to both communicate mission and build relationships.

Younger donors, in general, like very much to be connected to other donors whose interests are similar to their own. It is part of why social networks like Facebook have become havens for political and community organizing. This can work in favor of or against the church. The church can link members of the congregation around similar issues, help them to donate, and help them to form small communities of interest that promise to benefit everyone.

So what can a church do to improve giving by younger people in general?

Making the Link with Younger Members

1. Register your church with volunteer networks that do hands-on work in the community and the world, and build your own volunteer system to get people physically engaged on days other than Sundays.

2. Connect to your younger donors and members online through Facebook, MySpace, Twitter and other developing social media. On Facebook you can even use a program called "causes" to connect donors to friends and charities that do good work.

3. Use a blog and an e-news blast to keep younger people informed about what you are doing. Be sure to maintain the page, refreshing it almost daily and keeping it accurate and full of a spirit that will energize your donors.

4. Bring younger people in the congregation into leadership, whether via the vestry or other key decision-making bodies. If you have the opportunity to elect a youth to Diocesan Convention, by all means do so . . . and then welcome them to present to the whole congregation. If you have a youth or young adult group, create a "council of advice" to the vestry so that their voices can be heard and honored.

5. Look at all branding and marketing with an eye toward younger members. Better yet, get their input on drafts, images, tag lines, headlines and plans.

6. Always ask yourself as you manage your stewardship pledge campaign, "Is this 'ask' based on our needs or on the donors' mission? Have we communicated our mission so well and so involved our young people in our leadership that they own the mission of this church?" If the answer is no, then you have work to do.

CONCLUSION

I pray that there will come a time when nobody will need to buy this book.

If and when that time comes, there will neither be stewardship sermons nor pledge cards, neither fundraising nor campaign letters. This time will come when we all know how desperately God loves us. As Paul put it, "For now we see in a mirror, dimly, but then we will see face to face. Now I know only in part; then I will know fully, even as I have been fully known" (1 Corinthians 13:12).

In fact the whole point of our faith is that God came to be among us in Jesus and *remained* among us in the Holy Spirit. God is no absentee landowner. God, who loves us—even likes us—is here among us. We are not stewards as much as we are guests.

When we open our eyes to this reality, we will see the world as it truly is. We will see the disparity between rich and poor, and it will break our hearts open. We will see that God's holiness is outside the walls of our beloved churches. We will turn from entertainment that blocks mindfulness, and we will set down the self-anesthetizing addictions with which we dull our response to the world's and our own pain.

When we see face-to-face the God who is nearly crazy with love for us, we will loosen the death grip we have on our resources, and there will no longer be a need to raise money—it will flow so freely that the church will have a crisis about how to spend it.

If this book does nothing else, it will, I hope and pray, blow away the smoke of over-spiritualized mumbo-jumbo to expose a people longing to be healed from the fear and self-loathing the church has inspired in them as a chief means of raising money. It has been our reality for more than fifty generations. But it does not have to continue.

God does not want our money. God wants our whole selves. Our pledge is just a symbol that we understand the situation. Our pledge to the church is our way of being in community with each other. Our pledge is our way of showing God that we are grateful for all God has given us. Our pledge is our contract with God—a way of being released to spend the rest of our money joyfully.

When we finally come to see how loved we are by God, when we finally come to see how wonderful life is and how blessed we are, when we finally come to be able to express our gratitude—then and only then will we give our money, without struggle, to God through the church. And when that day comes, stewardship campaigns and ministries will become extinct like the dodo bird.

Fearless church fundraising is about exchanging fear for awe. When we do that our disordered lives will find order, our dull churches will find excitement, and our concerns over money will be enveloped in God's mission of reconciliation.

The One Thing

I was once asked at a conference what I would suggest a church do to prepare for a more effective stewardship program. I suppose they thought I would pick from the Bible or from some great book by a church mystic about bounty or generosity. Perhaps they wanted me to ask them to memorize the passages where Jesus spoke of money.

I could see the surprise on their face when I suggested two things that would transform their stewardship program from the inside out.

First, I suggested that they observe three three-minute periods of absolute silence in their liturgy. Three minutes of silence in our society will feel like a long time, and three of them will have many a vestry at the priest's door with torches and pitchforks. But it is in this silence that the Holy Spirit will do her best work, and it is in this silence that she will get a word in edgewise.

Silence is the foundation of awareness. Our members come to church craving this stillness, and more often than not they leave our churches unsatiated.

Second, I suggested the church read and pray with this passage from *The Wind in the Willows* by Kenneth Grahame, because if we can return to being transfigured by the glory of God, everything else, including church fundraising, will fall neatly into place.

> Then suddenly, the Mole felt a great Awe fall upon him, an awe that turned his muscles to water, bowed his head, and rooted his feet to the ground. It was no panic—indeed he felt wonderfully at peace and happy—but it was an awe that smote and held him . . . (He) raised his humble head; and

then, in that utter clearness of the imminent dawn . . . he looked into the
very eyes of the Friend and Helper . . . and still, as he looked, he lived; and
still, as he lived, he wondered.

"Rat," he found breath to whisper shaking. "Are you afraid?"

"Afraid?" murmured the Rat, his eyes shining with unutterable love,
"Afraid! Of HIM? O never, never! And yet—and yet—oh, Mole, I am
afraid!"

Then the two animals, crouching to the earth, bowed their heads and
did worship." [6]

This kind of fear is not rooted in terror but rather in awe, the kind that
inclines people to give their whole lives to God's movement happening
within and outside the church. This new kind of fear is not about hellfire
but is about working with intention and compassion to transform a world.
Gone are the days of clergy building empires. This is a fresh, new day, and
it calls for a new way of raising money based in awesome glory and not
fearful wrath.

We need not be afraid of the process of raising money. You know by now
how simple it is:

1. Deserve the money you are trying to raise
2. Deepen the spiritual lives of the people from whom you seek
   to raise it
3. Convert churchgoers from passive to active members of a
   church family
4. Drop the anxiety and add some fun to the process.

The only fear to which we are called is a holy, life-changing, awe-filled
fear in the full, bright, transfiguring presence of a living God whose mission
we long to make our own. It is a fear and awe that burns away the old selves
and the old fears, and allows us to become more and more the people of
resurrection joy.

One day, we will so heal from the lies the church has told us for centuries
about how bad we are and how angry God is at our sins that we will come
to the full knowledge of our goodness. And then we will come to the full
knowledge that we are basically good and streaked with evil—not the reverse. When we know we are good and when we know we are loved, we will
give and pledge. Until then, as we deepen our spiritual lives, fundraising will

---

6. Kenneth Grahame, *The Wind in the Willows* (New York: Charles Scribner's Sons,
1908), 161–63, quoted in Robert Morris, *Weavings: A Journal of the Christian Spiritual
Life* (Nashville: The Upper Room, 1999), XIV, 2 (March/April 1999): 21–29.

assist us in this good work of living into our Imago Dei—our Divine Image as lovers, creators and self-offerers.

One day, our churches will be so joyful, our sermons so well-preached and our lives so transformed that there will be no need for fundraisers or stewardship campaigns. Until then, however, we work and we pray and we use the resources available to us—prayerbooks, hymnals and books like the one you are holding in your hands right now. God bless us everyone indeed!